# SAINT JOSEPH

## *Patron of the Triumph*

Fr. Richard Foley, S.J.

Queenship

**PUBLISHING COMPANY**
P.O. Box 220 • Goleta, CA 93116
(800) 647-9882 • (805) 692-0043 • Fax: (805) 967-5133

Library of Congress Number # 02-141052

Published by:
Queenship Publishing
P.O. Box 220
Goleta, CA 93116
(800) 647-9882 • (805) 692-0043 • Fax: (805) 967-5133
http://www.queenship.org

Printed in the United States of America

ISBN: 1-57918-178-3

# CONTENTS

# DEDICATION

To my Jesuit confrere, JPD, at whose suggestion
I set about writing this book and with whose
encouragement I completed it.

# FOREWORD

D uring the Fatima solar miracle of October 13, 1917, St. Joseph appeared with the Child Jesus and blessed the world. The following is the account of Sr. Lucia from her *Memoirs:*

> "After Our Lady had disappeared into the immense distance of the firmament, we beheld St. Joseph with the Child Jesus and Our Lady robed in white with a blue mantle, beside the sun. St. Joseph and the Child Jesus appeared to bless the world, for they traced the sign of the cross with their hands."

This Josephite event is only understandable in light of the heart of the Fatima message, revealed on July 13, 1917. Our Lady of the Rosary revealed that following grave global event, inclusive of the worldwide spread of the error of Communism, a conditional second world war, the annihilation of various nations, and much suffering for the Holy Father and the Church, that eventually, "in the end, My Immaculate Heart will triumph" and "a period of peace would be granted to the world."

Of what then, does this Triumph of the Immaculate Heart consist? Amidst the great range of revelations and speculations in answer to this question, there remains a foundational pillar. The Triumph of the Immaculate Heart must lead to a spiritual renewal of the Eucharistic Jesus within the Church, and from the Church to the world. Without such spiritual renewal of the Heart of Jesus Christ in the Church and thus the world, the Mother's Heart, totally given to the adoration of His and the sanctification of ours, could never triumph victoriously. For the Immaculate Heart to triumph, so too must the Church, the Mystical Body of Her Son.

When Bl. Pope Pius IX declared St. Joseph the "Patron of the Universal Church" in 1870, he prophetically gave answer to the question of Joseph's presence at Fatima. *The Triumph of the Immaculate Heart is a spiritual Triumph of the Church, and the greatest intercessor for the Church, after the Mediatrix of all graces, is he who is the spiritual Foster Father of the Church.* Simply put, **St. Joseph is the Patron of the Triumph of the Immaculate Heart of Mary.**

Augustinian wisdom regarding St. Joseph and the Mystical Body leads to the conclusion that as St. Joseph was to Jesus, so is St. Joseph to the members of His Body, of which Jesus is the Head. Rightly therefore, is St. Joseph to be considered by every Christian as our own spiritual Foster Father, laden with great powers of intercession by his Divine Foster Son to assist us in every daily event, both spiritual and temporal.

It stretches the imagination to ponder the virtues and gifts given by Abba Father to Joseph enabling him to act, at least in part, as Abba's human replacement on earth in paternal love and care for the Word made flesh. As St. Thomas Aquinas reminds us, we are given all graces necessary to fulfill the responsibilities of our God-given vocations on earth, and when your earthly vocation is to be the foster father and faithful guardian of the Word Incarnate, and as well the chaste spouse of Mary Co-redemptrix, the graces to fulfill such vocation are inestimable.

The daily praying of the Litany of St. Joseph brings to life and love these remarkable virtues which are also so crucially needed for pursuing holiness in the 21st century. The "Mirror of Patience," "Glory of Home Life" and "Safeguard of Families" guides every sincere Christian husband and wife in the formation of their domestic church. The "Lover of Poverty," "Solace of the Afflicted" and "Joseph Most Obedient" offer holy direction and example to every priest and religious. And the "Terror of the Demons" awakens and re-directs the drifting mind of every half-slumbering child during family prayer to the dynamic and powerful spiritual effects of the intercession of St. Joseph in the spiritual warfare of today.

But to fully tap the rich reservoir of Josephite intercession for our lives and our families we must deliberately and consistently open our minds and hearts to our God-given Foster Father.

In this regard, we owe a wealth of thanks and appreciation to

Fr. Richard Foley, S.J. for this work, an outstanding labor of love offered for the edification of both head and heart regarding our beloved St. Joseph. A renowned international author, Fr. Foley with his exceptional gifts of articulation and commentary offers the reader a concise but bountiful synthesis of the pearls of saints and scholars regarding the greatest saint after the Immaculate One, he who can rightly be called "blessed among men." This work reminds one of the great insight of Venerable Cardinal Newman, that sound doctrinal material tends by its very nature to generate a corresponding devotion in the well-disposed hearer.

You will be richly blessed by opening your minds and heart to the wisdom contained in *St. Joseph, Patron of the Triumph*. May your devotion to St. Joseph only continue to crescendo during this brief earthly pilgrimage, until your own "face to face" meeting with your spiritual Foster Father in the Heavenly Jerusalem.

Dr. Mark Miravalle
Professor of Theology and Mariology
Franciscan University of Steubenville
August 5, 2001 *Feast of Our Lady of Snows*

CHAPTER ONE

# MAN OF DESTINY

Nobody has understood better than Teresa of Avila what a leading figure St Joseph is in the story of redemption and how powerful is his intercession in heaven. Nor has anybody done more than the great Spanish Carmelite to promote devotion to the saint. What started her on this programme was a sensational healing she herself experienced through St Joseph's intercession; she had been stricken when still in her twenties with a devastating paralysis that held nearly her entire body in its grip. Finally she had recourse to St Joseph—and was completely cured. Her gratitude and zeal on behalf of her new-found patron were glowingly recorded in her Autobiography: [1]

"I wish I could persuade everyone to be devoted to the glorious St Joseph, for I have great experience of the blessings which he can obtain from God. I do not remember that I have ever asked anything of him which he has failed to grant. I am astonished at the great favours which God has bestowed on me through this blessed saint, and at the perils from which he has delivered me, both in body and in soul.

"To other saints the Lord seems to have given grace to succour us in some of our necessities. But my experience is that St Joseph succours us in them all; also that the Lord wishes to teach us that, as He was himself subject on earth to St Joseph, so in Heaven He now does all that Joseph asks. This has also been the experience of other persons whom I have advised to commend themselves to the saint."

## St Joseph is Unique

St Joseph's mighty intercessory power reflects, of course, his exalted status as guardian of "God's two most precious treasures," as John Paul II calls Jesus and Mary.[2] In the very nature of things, Joseph's joint paternal and conjugal role brought him into a close family relationship with the God-Man and his mother. Indeed, the saint's intimate proximity to them in a domestic setting, and for so long a time, is nothing less than awesome to contemplate.

With good reason, then, Christian tradition has from the beginning honoured the Saviour's guardian as being not only sublimely privileged but supremely holy—the next-holiest, in fact, after his immaculate spouse. "Singular and utterly incomparable" is how Pius XI described the saint's holiness.[3]

Another ardent devotee—Cardinal Newman[4]—notes that the head of the Holy Family achieved such a degree of holiness because of his long and close communion with "the Source of all holiness and the holiest of his creatures."

## A Powerful Patron

So it is with good reason that Christ's virginal father has always been venerated as a mega-star in the firmament of God's holy ones and possesses a correspondingly exceptional power of intercession. Which power is further enhanced by the deep mutual love that binds him now and forever to the God of grace and the Mother of Divine Grace.

This last point was highlighted by John Gerson—a distinguished medieval theologian and ardent St Joseph devotee. After assuring us that the saint lovingly receives our petitions and recommends them to Jesus and Mary, Gerson exclaims:[5]

**"What a great intercessor is Joseph! For it is as a husband that he pleads with his spouse, and as a father that he appeals to his Son. Nay, more than that, he commands him! Hence his prayers on our behalf are always answered."**

Another ardent devotee—St Francis of Sales—exhorts us in similar fashion. "Our Blessed Lady and her glorious Son," he declares, "will refuse Joseph nothing." [6]

Nor are Teresa and Francis of Sales the only canonized saints to have practised and propagated a special devotion to the spouse of the Virgin Mary. A whole galaxy of God's holy ones across the centuries have done likewise, including such illustrious names as Benedict, Bernard, Francis of Assisi, Dominic, Ignatius Loyola, John of the Cross, Peter Canisius, Bernardine and Catherine of Siena, Alphonsus Liguori, Bernadette, and Teresa of Lisieux.

Special mention is merited in this context of an outstanding devotee of St Joseph in modern times—"Brother Andre" of Montreal; he was beatified in 1984. Through his ardent and lifelong promotion of the saint's cultus, which was backed up by multiple healings and other miracles (all of which the humble lay-brother attributed to his great patron), he touched literally millions of lives in Canada and abroad. Moreover, he founded St Joseph's Oratory in Montreal; on a world-wide scale it now serves to bring St Joseph into countless hearts and homes.

### St Joseph's Mission

Leo XIII says of Joseph's part in salvation history: [7]

> **"His was a unique and magnificent mission: namely, that of protecting not only the Son of God and King of the World but also Mary's virginity and holiness. It was the singular mission of entering into participation in the great mystery hidden from the eyes of past ages, and thus of cooperating in the Incarnation and Redemption."**

This text supplies the underlying reason for Joseph's pre-eminence and prerogatives: he was Mary's husband besides legal father and protector of the Christ-Child she miraculously conceived. Consequently, as the pontiff went on to say, "Joseph stands out among all the saints in his august dignity."

He does indeed. It could even be said that the carpenter of Nazareth's distinguished role renders him as blessed among menfolk as Mary is among women. For his sacred task was no less than to ensure that God's redemptive purposes went according to plan by protecting and providing for the Redeemer and the Co-redemptrix. Joseph was the chosen soul entrusted by the Father with their custody and care—the chosen soul whom Scripture virtually canonized by designating him a "just man" (Mt 1: 19).

## Joseph Was Indispensable

Essentially, then, Joseph's lifework was to cooperate, at the next highest level below that of Mary, in the greatest of God's works—the Incarnation of the Second Person of the Trinity as Redeemer of fallen mankind. Indeed, Joseph's cooperation in becoming Mary's spouse was indispensable if the Son of God was to enter our human world within the conventional framework of marriage and family life.

Also imperative to the providential plan was that the Child and his virgin mother should have, right from the outset, a reliable protector, guide, and breadwinner; otherwise they would scacely have coped with the perils, needs, hazards, challenges and crosses lying ahead in the shadows of the future.

Again, the Christ-Child would benefit by that specific contribution which normally only a father can make towards a balanced upbringing and social development. Furthermore, the paternal input in Joseph's case would later include the divine Child's training as a carpenter, so preparing him for the day when he would sanctify the world of work and of earning one's living.

## Joseph's Preparation

So Joseph is far from being a merely ornamental or even peripheral figure in the drama of Jesus. Morover, such was the dignity of his office and the huge responsibilities devolving from it that very special qualities of mind and character were clearly called for. Providence accordingly endowed him with all the requisite gifts, both natural and supernatural. For it is a theological axiom that, when God selects certain individuals for a special function, he duly equips them with the wherewithal to perform it worthily and well.

It goes without saying, of course, that Joseph's cooperation in the divine plan hinged in the first place on his full consent, since God unfailingly respects the noble gift of free will enjoyed by his human images. And Joseph's consent was implicit in his prompt and unquestioning execution of the angel's instructions; namely, that he should go ahead with his marriage to Mary rather than seek a divorce (cf. Mt 1: 19-21).

Thus the saint was caught up, jointly with his spouse, into the Eternal Father's merciful designs for our fallen world when he sent his Word-Son to be one of its citizens—and victimal Redeemer. Thus, too, as we have seen, the way was paved for Jesus to be born in lawful wedlock and grow up in a family milieu. Furthermore, thanks to his legal father's Davidic ancestry, he could vindicate his Messianic claim to be descended from the same royal lineage.

### The Word Made Flesh

**"Joseph, Son of David, do not be afraid to take thy wife Mary to thyself, for it is by the power of the Holy Spirit that she has conceived this child; and she will bear a son, whom thou shalt call Jesus, for he is to save his people from their sins" (Mt 1:20-21).**

St Joseph rightly understood from the angel's words, as Mary had done at the Annunciation, that the Child conceived virginally in her womb was the long-awaited Messiah, the Son of the Most High. Equivalently, therefore, both spouses affirmed their faith in the mighty mystery of the Incarnation, whereby the Second Person of the Trinity united himself with the human nature he assumed in and from his mother. The Word was made Flesh. God became Incarnate. The Son of the Eternal Father became Emmanuel—God with us.

What this profound mystery signifies is that Godhead and manhood became now and forever fused, as it were, into that unitary, personal Being we know and adore as Jesus of Nazareth. And this took place, let it be said again, thanks to the all-important roles played respectively by Mary and Joseph.

As result and reward this chosen couple, through being involved as leading figures in the Incarnation, acquired the supreme honour of belonging in a highly privileged way to human redemption— Mary directly so by conceiving the Divine Person in her womb, her spouse indirectly as an integral participant in the proceedings. To quote a prayer from the Votive Mass in his honour, "St Joseph helped to carry out the great mysteries of our salvation."

The principal contribution to these great mysteries came, of course, from the God-Man's virgin mother; as for St Joseph's, vital though it was, it remained secondary and subordinate throughout to the Virgin Mother's.

### Salvation is the Aim

An all-important word in this whole context is "salvation." For it was to this end and purpose that the Incarnation was directed in the first place. In other words, God's motivation and goal was to restore its supernatural destiny to our fallen world, as the angel made clear to St Joseph: "Thou shalt call him Jesus, for he is to save his people from their sins" (Mt 1: 21).

A further consequence of the Incarnation is that Jesus's parents, through being locked into it from the start, were destined to play in the centuries to come an ongoing role in bringing its fruits to mankind. Which role is strikingly verified in the fact that Mary and Joseph now function as mother and universal patron respectively of the Church founded by their Redeemer-Son to bring his salvation to successive generations.

To put this another way, there is a prominent apostolic dimension to the positions of both Mary and Joseph, as John Paul II so clearly recognises. Hence his frequent allusions to Mary as Mother of the Church and Queen of Apostles. Similarly, in his stirring apostolic exhortation on St Joseph he urges us, as we progress into the new millennium, to imitate the zeal for souls that burns in the heart of the Church's universal patron.

## The Saint's Background

The simple reason why anything like a proper biography of Joseph is entirely out of the question is that the available facts about his personal background and private circumstances are scanty in the extreme. Not even a single word he uttered bas been recorded; hence Claudel's famous dictum:[8] "The man of silence is father of the Word." Nevertheless, what is at least a recognizable and positive profile of the saint emerges from the gospel narratives; it is that of a man of action, practical, dedicated, single-minded, self-effacing, totally faithful and devout in his service of the divine will.

Wherefore Scripture has coined an even more famous dictum, applying to the Virgin Mary's spouse the lapidary compliment: "a just man" (Mt I: 19). Which, as we noted earlier, virtually amounts in biblical usage to the equivalent of canonization.

As has also been noted, we do happen to know one highly significant fact about Joseph's own distinguished, indeed royal, pedigree: namely, he was by descent a "son of David," which was a defining title for any would-be Messianic claimant; therefore as Christ's putative father he transmitted to him a like juridical claim to descent from Davidic lineage.

## Joseph, Splendour of Patriarchs

A further distinction belonging to Joseph is that he virtually embodied in himself the entire Old Testament heritage besides bridging it with the New. As a devout Israelite he yearned for the coming of the promised Messiah. And as the man chosen by God to be the yearned-for One's father and guardian, Joseph was to behold with his own eyes, lying helpless in the Bethlehem manger, the living fulfilment of Israel's Messianic hopes and expectations—the King of Kings and Lord of Lords, the Desire of the Eternal Hills, the Prince of Peace and Father of the World to Come, Jesus, Mighty God.

So St Joseph is rightly hailed in the litany as "the splendour of patriarchs." Included in that illustrious Old Testament dynasty was the saint's great namesake, Patriarch Joseph, the son of Jacob, who was destined to become Viceroy of Egypt. From Christianity's early days he has been recognized as the prototype and prefigurement of the Patriarch of Nazareth, and this on a number of counts, including his name, his heroic chastity, his innocence and grace, and the many rich favours he received from God.

Among other prefiguring features between the two Josephs are the following: both fled to Egypt; both received supernatural communications through the medium of dreams; both supplied bread for the people in time of famine—one with material bread, the other in his guardianship of the Living Bread that came down from Heaven.

## From Shadows to Limelight

The earliest Christian art as found in the Roman catacombs portrays Joseph at the time of his marriage to Mary as a fine, upstanding young man—which he almost certainly was. But this image started to change somewhat drastically in the fourth century.

Mary's husband was now being widely portrayed instead as a man advanced in years, stooped and balding; those responsible for the new-look St Joseph were convinced that hereby they would help to shield his wife's virginal status now that it was being challenged and denied.

This new senile perception of St Joseph was also prominently propagated by the so-called apocryphal gospels—those spurious accounts of Our Lord's childhood and later years. Feeding as they did as much on fantasy as on fact (St Jerome dismissed them as "delirious nonsense"), these fictional writings indulged in wild and extravagant exaggerations, especially concerning legendary miracles performed by the Child Jesus.

In any case, during the first Christian millennium comparatively little public cultus was paid to St Joseph. This was undoubtedly due in great part due to the attention demanded by the defence and definition of key dogmatic truths concerning Christ and his mother.

Subsequently it was the influence of medieval saints and mystics that awakened a widespread interest in St Joseph and led to his liturgical cultus being developed. Leading figures like John Gerson, St Bernardine of Siena and, later, Sts Teresa of Avila and Francis of Sales played notable parts in spreading the devotion at a popular level.

Starting with Pius IX, who in 1870 proclaimed St Joseph universal patron of the Church,[9] a succession of modern pontiffs, notably Leo XIII, have promoted both private and public devotion to the Redeemer's father and guardian.

## St Joseph of Fatima

During her fourth apparition to the Fatima visionaries in 1917, the mother of God foretold that, on the coming October 13th, St Joseph would appear besides herself, and that he would be holding the Child Jesus in his arms. Which duly happened on what was to be her sixth and final apparition on October 13, 1917.

On that crowning occasion the Virgin exhorted the children to recite the rosary daily, to amend their lives, and to make frequent acts of contrition. Next came the stupendous miracle of the sun before the crowd of at least seventy thousand.

One of the visionaries, writing in later life as Sister Lucia, outlined events following the sun-miracle as follows. First Our Lady reappeared, robed in white with a blue mantle, and standing on the left of the sun.

Sister Lucia relates that they were then shown three successive scenes depicting the three parts of the rosary—the joyful, sorrowful and glorious mysteries. Prominently featured in the joyful mysteries was the red-mantled figure of St Joseph with the Christ-Child in his arms; positioned to the right of the sun, they jointly made the sign of the cross in blessing over the world.

What significance, we may wonder, does Our Lady of Fatima intend us to read into the Joseph-and-Child apparition? In the first place, she is drawing our attention to the commanding role her spouse played in the real-life joyful episodes, as well as encouraging us to recall his presence when we recite the rosary.

Secondly, she is highlighting the fact that her Fatima message addressed to the contemporary Church has the full support and blessing of its universal patron. That is to say, along with the Church's mother he underlines the need for prayer (notably the rosary) and penance, in order to obtain God's blessing on such issues as world peace, the conversion of Russia, and work for the salvation of souls.

## St Joseph and Theology

Shrouded though Joseph the man is in obscurity and silence, he is nonetheless one of the principal characters in the gospel story. Indeed, a special branch of theology has developed about him and his significance in the Christian scheme of things; technically known as Josephology, it is proving to be a goldmine of faith and devotion. That is why today more and more theologians and spiritual writers are coming to realise that "the man closest to Christ" casts many a searching sidelight on faith's mysteries, illumining them with a fresh radiance and significance.

To begin with Joseph's true marriage to Mary and their joint virginal parenthood of the Divine Child. From these themes alone flow any number of connected sub-themes, such as conjugal love, fatherhood, virginity, chastity, fidelity, the family, parental duties, filial obedience—all of which happen to be directly and even urgently relevant to contemporary society.

As for Joseph's role as breadwinner for the Holy Family, it naturally prompts us to reflect on the concept of work as such in the Creator's plan for mankind. Similarly the concept of death; its linkage with the saint derives from his being the time-honoured patron of a happy death. A further key subject linked with St Joseph is the Church, of which his Nazareth family was the nucleus and prototype, and over which he now holds universal patronage.

## Our Model and Master

A wide range of additional reflections and insights are sparked off by Joseph's life and experiences. These include the mystery of suffering, his tremendous faith and equally tremendous trust in divine providence, his total commitment to the divine will. All of which (and there are many more besides) contain profound lessons for us.

"Lessons"—here we have a defining keyword in our study of St Joseph. For he is essentially a role-model and teacher for all who aspire after Christian holiness. Let us recall that he himself was a star pupil in that great school of holiness founded in his Nazareth home by the Holy One of Israel, the Eternal Wisdom of the Father, who would later articulate his school's syllabus in the pages of the gospel and enroll us through baptism as his disciples.

It is within this particular area of the imitation of Christ and Christian spirituality in general that Joseph-inspired sub-themes multiply thick and fast. For Christian piety can identify in the "just man" of Nazareth every single virtue, each gift of the Holy Spirit, and all the beatitudes.

Space considerations obviously oblige us to confine our attention throughout these pages to those specific sub-themes which in one way and another have a more practical bearing on our spiritual lives.

### REFERENCES FOR CHAPTER ONE
### MAN OF DESTINY

1...St Teresa of Avila: Autobiography, ch 6
2...John Paul II: Redemptoris Custos, I
3...Pius XI: Discourse, 19 March 1928
4...Cardinal John Henry Newman: Meditations and Devotions
5...John Gerson: Opera Omnia, V. 356
6...St Francis of Sales: Discourse 19 in Complete Works of
    St Francis of Sales, VI
7...Leo XIII: Quamquam Pluries
8...Paul Claudel: Positions et Propositions, vol 2, 147
9...Pius IX: Quemadmodum Deus

St. Joseph, Patron of the Triumph

CHAPTER TWO

# SPOUSE OF THE VIRGIN MARY

S t Augustine's formula goes to the very heart of the matter. "Joseph," he said, "is everything he is through Mary and because of Mary."[1] What this tells us is that the saint's whole meaning and mission consist in his being spouse of Mary and legal father of her Divine Child. These roles are the twin pillars upon which rests everything we believe and venerate about the Carpenter of Nazareth. Therefore, to get him more sharply into focus, we must consider his august status within the Holy Family as its spouse and father. We begin with the former.

## A Marriage Made in Heaven

If ever the saying applied literally to a marriage, it was the Mary-Joseph one. Though virginal from start to finish, it was providentially planned to produce the Infant Messiah as its fruit and offspring. Nor did the perpetual virginity of both partners in any way diminish, still less invalidate, their married status or their true parenthood. Again St Augustine supplies us with a tailor-made text: [2]

> **"Just as Mary was virginally Joseph's wife, so was he virginally her husband. And just as she was virginally the mother, so was he virginally the father ... The Holy Spirit gave the Divine Child to both of them."**

Belonging to each other as a wedded couple, Mary and Joseph consequently owned everything in common, not least the all-precious Offspring given them by God. Their deep mutual love now found its highest fulfilment in the Divine Child. Or as Leo XIII [3] said of this mystery: "The consummation of their love was in Jesus."

## Love's Young Dream

It was conjugal love, of course, that bonded Mary and Joseph. And, in conformity with normal Jewish custom, their marital union would have been preceded by a period of courtship. Doubtless it had been a case of love at first sight between the innocent girl from Nazareth and her spouse-to-be. Anyhow they fell in love with one another and became a courting couple, thus experiencing for themselves something of the glad surprise, the excitement, the tenderness and intense human joy so well expressed in the lines:

> **"No, there's nothing half so sweet in life
> As love's young dream."**[4]

So this chosen pair, who were destined to stand at the threshold of the New Testament as commandingly as our first parents did at the Old, sanctified for all time the love of courtship as they would subsequently do in respect of marital and parental love. By being caught up in the tender mysteries of romantic love they raised "the holiness of the heart's affections" to sublime heights. We can assume that a deep mutual empathy instinctively arose between the young couple, an empathy born of their instant recognition in each other of Israel's high and holy ideals. Michael O'Carroll has written with delicate sensitivity about their early relationship:

> **"This ideal of love was realised between Mary and Joseph through their total acceptance of the primacy of spirit. It was love stripped of all those ignoble things that lessen it. It was love as a form of communion between two persons, each endowed with a delicate and heroic reverence for the other. Yet it was not in spirit alone that they loved. Their physical nature they had consecrated, and thus their bodily appetites, elevated by chastity, became, as it were, sacramentals. The tenderness which accompanies love on the physical plane was not a prelude to physical union. It was for them a symbol, the external sign, of spirit and of grace."[5]**

Little though the gracious young couple were aware of it at the time, their love's young dream would before long lead to the fulfilment of another dream—one altogether vast and momentous in import. It was nothing less than the Chosen People's long-cherished dream of the Messiah-Redeemer due to be born of a virgin mother. The stage was now being set for that dream to come true, and Mary and Joseph were heaven's chosen instruments in its realisation. The kingdom of the God-Man was at hand, imminently so. The virgin of Nazareth and her spouse would shortly be launching into this sinful world of ours the thousand mysteries of Jesus.

## Their Virginal Marriage

According to a steady tradition dating back to the Apostolic age, Mary and Joseph had each already made a lifelong vow of chastity; yet, this notwithstanding, they were subsequently prompted by the Holy Spirit to contract a virginal marriage.

We may note here that, following the example of these illustrious partners, virginal marriages would become fairly common among Christians from earliest times. And what these spouses intended thereby was to imitate the parents of Jesus by consecrating themselves more completely to God through the mutual renunciation of marriage rights.

It is patently false to claim, as some do, that Joseph and Mary's marriage was invalid through being virginal. The Church has always taught that the essence of marriage lies in the invisible union of souls effected by the partners' mutual consent. What constitutes a marriage, then, is the spiritual bond between husband and wife. As for marriage's consummation through sexual union (sometimes referred to as the use of marriage), important though it is, it nevertheless plays but a secondary role. Once again St Augustine can be called upon to supply an apposite text: [6]

**"Joseph is the husband of Mary, her partner in continence, not by carnal embrace but by affection, not by union of bodies but by what matters still more: the communion of their souls. Faithful married couples**

> may learn from their example that, if they practise continence by mutual consent, their marriage can remain and be called such if the affection of their minds is preserved even without the sexual union of their bodies."

## Marriage Ceremony

The Messiah's parents-to-be would have followed scrupulously the conventional procedures laid down by Jewish law and custom as regards getting married. The ceremonies involved were performed in two stages, the first of which, known as espousals, was in fact the operative factor in that it effectively made the couple husband and wife. Far from simply amounting to what we would call their engagement, a true and valid marriage was contracted when, at this first stage, the partners plighted their troth and exchanged conjugal rights.

The second stage of the marriage ceremony was its public celebration or solemnization. But this did not take place immediately, because Jewish custom required that a certain interval should intervene before the bride took up domicile with the bridegroom. The main reason behind this was that in many instances the bride was still a girl in her mid-teens. As for the length of this interval, it could stretch over a year or more, though commonly it was of shorter duration.

So stage two of the marriage ceremony was purely social in effect, its central feature being the bride's induction into her husband's home—thereafter to be her own home as well. On that journey she was ceremonially escorted in a procession led by a bevy of bridesmaids, and the occasion was marked by festive lights, music, dancing, revelry, and the provision of wine and refreshments.

Incidentally, the gospel refers on two occasions to such a wedding ceremony. The first was Our Lord's parable about the ten bridesmaids (Mt 25: 2-13), while the second featured the famous Cana episode that witnessed his first miracle, significantly performed at his mother's intervention.

## A Baffled Spouse

Mary and Joseph duly went through the stage-one ceremony, thereby becoming husband and wife in the eyes of the law and of the Lord alike. Now it was just a matter of waiting the agreed interval of time before Mary took up residence in Joseph's home.

However, it was precisely during this interval that a wholly unexpected development took place; it caused Joseph not only complete surprise but considerable shock as well. His wife was found to be with child. This baffled him all the more because of his unshaken conviction that Mary was chaste and innocent; moreover, like himself, she was bound by a vow of lifelong virginity. On this account the troubled spouse firmly dismissed from his mind the least suspicion of infidelity on Mary's part, though the agonising problem still remained unresolved: how had his cherished and all-pure spouse become pregnant in the first place?

What rendered the situation still more fraught was the fact that Mary's lips were sealed, since she felt that the awesome mystery of Emmanuel's miraculous presence in her womb was a secret—something far too sacred to be shared with anyone else but God alone. Sensitively aware though she was that her condition caused Joseph deep perplexity and pain of mind, the expectant young mother nevertheless remained serene and at peace, confident that the Lord who had brought this situation about in the first place would resolve it in his own good time.

## Joseph's Dilemma

St Matthew informs us that Joseph was naturally pondering what line of action he should take. Meanwhile there had been a further development in the already complex scenario: Mary's kinswoman Elizabeth had miraculously conceived a child despite being well beyond her child-bearing years.

Actually this new development brought a ray of light into Joseph's puzzled mind, even providing a possible clue to Mary's mysterious pregnancy. Was it, too, like Elizabeth's, of the miraculous order of things? Indeed, could his wife's miraculous conception even signify that she was that chosen daughter of Israel who was destined to conceive virginally and give birth to the long-promised Messiah? (cf Isaias 7: 14)

Whatever its specific origin, Mary's pregnancy, the worried spouse concluded, could not otherwise be accounted for than in terms of some high and holy purpose at work in her and through her. St Bernard[7] is surely right when he explains that Joseph, besides being filled with reverential awe, now felt that Mary's destiny was on too exalted a plane for him to play any further part in her life. The sacred orbit into which she had been drawn by her miraculous conception was clearly above and beyond his own station in life. How, then, could he possibly expect someone so intimately caught up in God's designs to share his home and his life? Heartbreaking though the decision facing him was, he planned to obtain a divorce privately and without delay.

We know the sequel. God sent an angel to bring immediate enlightenment and consolation to the troubled man:

> **"Joseph, son of David, do not be afraid to take Mary, your wife, for that which is conceived in her is of the Holy Spirit; she will bear a son, and you shall call his name Jesus, for he will save his people from their sins"** (Mt 1: 18-21)

The saint's agonizing ordeal was borne away by the tidal wave of peace and joy that flooded his soul. Mary, too, rejoiced greatly as she prepared to share conjugal domicile with him who, to her vast relief, now shared her precious secret.

### Reasons for their Marriage

Why the virginal marriage was of such crucial importance is that it provided the basic human infrastructure for the divine adventure we know as the Incarnation. Nobody has understood this better than St Thomas; he advances no less than twelve reason why the Mary-Joseph union was indispensable for God's saving initiative.[8]

Four of these reasons focused directly on Christ himself. They establish that hereby the stigma of illegitimacy would be avoided;

that his Davidic descent would be ensured; that his helpless early years would be protected; and that his upbringing would benefit from St Joseph's fatherly love and instruction.

The Virgin Mary was the focus of St Thomas's next three reasons why her marriage to Joseph served an indispensable need. Hereby she would be immune from the legal penalty of stoning for which unmarried mothers were liable; likewise she would be spared the inevitable dishonour and defamation; and, thirdly, she and her Child would be protected and provided for by her spouse in the years ahead.

The remaining five reasons bear directly on ourselves and the Church. Mary and Joseph's marital union, besides reinforcing our belief in her virginal conception, acts as a type of the mystical marriage between Christ and his Church. Besides, Mary's conjugal union with Joseph demonstrates that virginity and motherhood co-exist in her as they do in the Lord's Mystical Bride.

### Did They Have Other Children?

Critics of the virginal marriage between Joseph and Mary commonly raise the above question. So we need to deal with it decisively if we are to have a clear picture of Christ's human background and St Joseph's place in it. It is on seemingly sound Scriptural grounds that the objection is based. Speaking of St Joseph, Luke writes: "He did not know her till she brought forth her first-born son" (2: 21) But does this not equivalently state that they lived together like any ordinary couple and went on to produce further offspring? Otherwise why does the evangelist speak of Mary's "first-born"? Besides, he evidently implies that, following the birth of their first-born, Joseph "knew" his wife, which in biblical parlance signifies carnal intercourse.

Joining forces with this objection is the other gospel phrase "the brothers of the Lord." Indeed, two evangelists even name four of these brothers (cf. Mt 13: 55; Mk 4: 3). Therefore are we not to assume that Mary's virginal conception, as well as her perpetual virginity, are nothing more than pious myths?

## The Meaning of "First-Born"

To refute these objections, we begin by noting that, in biblical usage, "first-born" (Lk 2: 6) does not necessarily imply that further offspring ensued. One of the greatest scholars of all time in this field—St Jerome—states definitively that in Sacred Scripture the term "first-born" designates "not only one after whom there are others but one after whom there are none." [9] And scores of eminent authorities testify in similar vein.

Furthermore, "first-born" in biblical usage simply indicates that this particular child is the one entitled to the privileges provided by the Mosaic law, such as a special consecration to the Lord by being presented to him in the temple (cf. Lk 2: 23).

A well-known biblical scholar [10] cites the case of a Jewish burial inscription dating from around the time of Christ's birth. It tells of a woman who had died "in the pangs of giving birth to a first-born child"—a clear indication that this was, in fact, her only one. Interestingly enough, another well-known biblical scholar [11] has pointed out that in medical parlance at that time "primipara" (first-born) could refer to the birth of a woman's first child without any implications as regards further offspring. And he makes the further point that elsewhere in the New Testament "first-born" happens to be applied to Christ's relationship to the Father (cf. Col 1: 15; Heb 1: 6; Apoc 1: 5).

Regarding the relationship between Mary and Joseph, the gospel phrase "he did not know her till she brought forth her first-born son" by no means implies (as the preposition "till" suggests) that subsequently they had marital intercourse. In several Scriptural texts can be found the selfsame idiomatic use of "till." For example, the raven sent out by Noah from the Ark did not return "till the waters had dried"—meaning, it never returned at all (cf. Gen 8: 70). Another example features Michol, the daughter of Saul. Of her it was written: "She had no child till the day of her death" (2 Kings 6: 23). Which obviously does not mean that she gave birth on her deathday.

## Brothers of the Lord

Biblical scholars are practically unanimous that this phrase really means "the cousins of the Lord." What gave rise to the ambivalence in the first place was the limited vocabulary of the original languages. John Paul II has clarified this point:[12]

> **"It should be recalled that no specific term exists in Hebrew or Aramaic to express the word "cousin," and that the terms "brother" and "sister" therefore had a far broader meaning which included several degrees of relationship."**

Scholars further point out that nowhere is it actually claimed that the Lord's so-called brothers were Mary's children or Joseph's. Besides, the gospels make it very clear that the Holy Family comprised but three persons—Jesus, Mary and Joseph. And this remained unchanged all the way from Bethlehem till the end of their days in Nazareth.

Also to be rejected as totally unfounded is the claim that Joseph was twice married, elderly, and had fathered children by his first wife. The claim was made by the apocryphal gospels and drew this response from St Jerome:[13]

> **"Some follow the hallucinations of the apocryphal writers in imagining that the phrase 'brothers of the Lord' refers to the sons of Joseph by another wife. We, however, understand the phrase to refer not to sons of Joseph but to cousins of the Saviour, who were in actual fact sons of Mary, the aunt of Jesus. That cousins were sometimes called brothers all Scripture bears witness."**

# REFERENCES FOR CHAPTER TWO
## SPOUSE OF THE VIRGIN MARY

1...St Augustine: Sermo 51, PL 38, 351
2...St Augustine: ibid
3...Leo XIII: Neminem Fugit, 1892
4...Thomas Moore: Irish Melodies— "Love's Young Dream"
5...Michael O'Carroll, C.S.Sp: Son of David, p 41
6...St Augustine: loc. cit.
7...St Bernard: In Laudibus Virginis Mariae, Hom. 2
8...St Thomas: Summa Theol. 3, 29, 1
9...St Jerome: In Matt. 12: 40, 50
10..J.A. Fitzmyer: The Gospel According to Luke, 407-408
11..Larry M. Toschi, OSJ: St Joseph in Sacred Scripture, article in Symposium St Joseph and the Third Millennium, edited by Michael D. Griffin, OCD, p 38
12..John Paul II: Catechesis, 29 August 1996
13..St Jerome: loc. cit.

# CHAPTER THREE

# THE EARLY YEARS

"It was through the exercise of his fatherhood," John Paul II explains, "that Joseph was called to serve the person and mission of Jesus."[1] To put this another way, what defined the saint's role in God's salvific plan was his status as father of the Saviour.

At what point, we may ask ourselves, did Joseph effectively assume his fatherly duties? He did so on the day of his wedding celebration, which entailed the official reception of his bride into his home—and along with her, of course, the Divine Infant nestling in her womb. Both mother and unborn Child thereupon came directly under St Joseph's authority, care and guardianship. That is to say, from that moment he became head of the Holy Family.

Meanwhile, as an Advent prayer says, it was "with a love beyond all telling" that the Virgin Mary bore the Infant Christ in her womb. And, like every expectant mother, she looked forward with eager longing to the birth of her little one and the sheer joy of holding him in her arms for the first time. Which happy prospect, she and Joseph naturally assumed, would take place here in their home.

## Journey to Bethlehem

But, even with regard to the Holy Family itself, life was soon to show itself well capable of dealing out unwelcome surprises and setbacks. This particular one came in the shape of an edict from the Roman emperor ordering a population census in all his subject provinces, which included, of course, Palestine. Its inhabitants were thereby required to register in their family's ancestral place of origin. Which for Mary and Joseph was Bethlehem, the town traditionally linked with the prophet David, from whose royal house and family they were both descended.

Surely nothing could have been more awkward and untimely

for the young couple than this enforced journey coming at such a juncture. For Mary's pregnancy was by now already in its final term; in Belloc's phrase, it was "her month of heavy load." Yet she and her husband were nevertheless obliged to set out on the arduous southward journey to Bethlehem, much of it over hilly terrain and liable to take anything up to a week or longer. Joseph, the soul of solicitude for his wife, would have procured a donkey to transport her, while he did the journey on foot.

To make matters still more awkward, on arrival in Bethlehem the travel-weary couple ran into a serious problem as regards accommodation. There was no room for them in the inn; hereby is meant what in the Near East is known as the local khan—a stockade with open alcoves where rough sleeping quarters were available for travellers and their pack animals could be tethered for the night.

But in any case such inns offered little privacy—a paramount need for a woman about to bring a child into the world. St Joseph, who would have done all the exploring and negotiating, had little choice but to settle for a nearby cave ordinarily used as a refuge for cattle. Primitive and rough though it was, at least it afforded them the necessary shelter and seclusion.

## The Real-Life Christmas

"And Mary brought forth her first-born Son and laid him in a manger" (Lk 2: 7). Never till his dying day would St Joseph forget that wonderful moment when he beheld for the first time the Word Incarnate placed by his mother on the stone shelf that normally served as a feeding trough for cattle. Along with Mary he was the first to offer the prayer of adoration to the new-born God-Man lying so tiny and helpless in the manger. Sentiments similar to his would one day inspire Blessed Henry Suso to write: "See how sweetly silent Wisdom lies there and cannot even speak."

True classic as it is, the Nativity Scene never loses its pristine appeal and charm. The main focus, of course, is on the baby lying asleep in the manger or cradled in his mother's arms. She is the picture of motherly tenderness as she takes care of her little one, by turns feeding him, changing him, pressing him close to her bosom, covering him betweenwhiles with multitudes of kisses, and lullabying him to sleep. Well did St Thomas observe that God, the better to win our hard, sinful hearts to his love and service, presented us in the drama of Jesus with two scenes that are crowning masterpieces—this one at Bethlehem, the other at Calvary.

Presiding protectively all the while over the first of these divine masterpieces was the vigilant figure of St Joseph. He is fully aware of his awesome responsibiity towards his spouse and their Child—the precious gift given by God jointly to himself and Mary as the fruit of their virginal marriage.

## The Epiphany

Meanwhile the Bethlehem hills were alive with the sound of music—-angel-music made by the heavenly hosts serenading their new-born King with that first-ever Christmas carol: "Glory to God in the highest and peace to his people on earth."

Meanwhile, too, an angel had appeared to shepherds watching over their flocks on a nearby hillside. His message was sensational and joyous: "In the city of David a Saviour has been born for you, the Lord Christ himself" (Lk 2: 10-11). He added that the sign whereby they would identify the location was the presence of "a child wrapped in swaddling-clothes and laid in a manger" (Lk 2: 12).

Joseph was subsequently to witness the adoration paid so humbly and devoutly by these shepherds to the Infant Saviour. What he would likewise witness in due course was the adoration of the Magi—those wise men from the East who had been guided by a mysterious star all the way to the new-born King's birthplace. As for the gifts they brought—gold, frankincense and myrrh—they were gratefully acknowledged and taken charge of by St Joseph.

Little could he have realised at the time how profoundly symbolical were these two contrasting sets of visitors paying the homage of adoration to the Divine Infant. The shepherds represented the people of Israel, the race chosen by God to give the fallen human race its Messiah. The wise men from the East, on the other hand, having been supernaturally enlightened, as the Fathers of the Church maintain, about the Child's divinity, stood proxy for the vast and varied non-Jewish world. The Fathers also see in the God-Man's early epiphany or manifestation to these visitors, all drawn by divine grace to the Nativity scene, the first direct exercise of God's redemptive mission to mankind.

## Tale of Two Cities

At the earliest opportunity after the birth of Jesus, his legal father would have fulfilled what had been the prime purpose of their coming down to Bethlehem in the first place: the registration of himself, his wife, and now also their Son in the census imposed by the ruling Roman authority.

Thus it came about that the entry "Jesus, son of Joseph of Nazareth" was officially entered by the saint in the population register of the Roman Empire. Many authors have drawn attention to the deep significance underlying this episode, none more illuminatingly so than Origen in the second century. "By being registered with everyone," he writes, "Jesus was in a position to sanctify everyone."[2]

John Paul II takes up this same theme.[3] The Saviour's inclusion in the census, he declares, enables him to identify fully with us as someone who belongs to the human race and is therefore a citizen of the world, subject like everyone else to human laws and civil institutions. In a word, the Son of God is very much the Son of Man as well. Founder and King of the eternal City of God though he is, now he is nonetheless a registered citizen of the unabiding City of Man. Through his humanity he renders due homage to God and Caesar alike.

But the whole point about that tiny Infant's inscription by Joseph into the census-roll of Caesar's subjects is that he is Founder and King of the eternal City of God. And into its register are entered the names of all his followers down the ages. Consequently St Paul can affirm that the "saints," whether they be already in heaven or still on earth, are fellow-citizens in the City of God (cf. Eph 2: 19). Thanks to the Holy One of Israel's having been added by his legal father to the imperial register that distant day in Bethlehem, we can look forward to eternal citizenship in the heavenly city. Prominent among its citizens are his loving parents, whose collaboration in God's designs made all this possible in the first place.

## The Circumcision

A further paternal right-cum-duty falling to Joseph by Mosaic law was to supervise the circumcision of the Infant Jesus eight days after his birth. God had made this rite a sign of his covenanted priestly people (Gen 17: 10) and strictly enjoined it on Abraham's progeny. Through undergoing this rite the infant became part of the people of the Covenant.

Through his circumcision the Saviour brought the Old Testament rite to its promised fulfilment, since his whole mission was to be the Mediator of the new and eternal covenant between God and man. Just as the Messianic prophecies find in him their consummation and goal, similarly he is in himself the Reality foreshadowed not only by circumcision but by all the Old Testament rites (cf. 2 Cor 1: 20; Acts 4: 12).

## The Name Above All Names

Also forming part of the circumcision ritual was the naming ceremony —a further duty binding exclusively on the father in question. Joseph duly conferred on the Christ-Child the name specified in the angel's instructions: "You shall call him Jesus, for he will save his people from their sins" (Mt 1: 21).

As Joseph knew full well, the name Jesus is Hebrew for "God saves." Herein, too, he saw a clear indication that it was precisely as our Saviour that the Lord was staging his Messianic adventure on mankind's behalf. Moreover, the Old Testament prophecies left no doubt that it was as a Suffering Messiah and Man of Sorrows that the Saviour would fulfil his mission.

Joseph witnessed during the circumcision rite the inevitable pain and bloodshed it caused the Infant. And he realised with sorrow that greater quantities of the precious blood were destined to be shed in the years to come. But the faithful guardian could scarcely have conceived what unspeakable sufferings did in fact lie ahead for the Saviour on Good Friday, the day when he would seal the new and everlasting covenant in his blood.

Jesus—the God who saves. Mary and Joseph would have reflected devoutly and frequently on how literal was their Son's name. He is not only called but **is** the God-sent Saviour. So "Jesus" should be for us, as it was for them, not merely a name but a prayer and an aspiration.

Devotion to the Holy Name was greatly promoted in the fifteenth century by two Franciscans, Saint Bernardine of Siena and John Capistran, both of whom were closely devoted to St Joseph. Indeed, it was largely this devotion that sparked their zeal for making known and honoured the name he conferred on the Divine Infant.

## The Presentation in the Temple

Forty days after the birth of Jesus, his parents duly took him to Jerusalem in compliance with another Mosaic law prescribing that first-born males were to be presented to the Lord in the temple. And on the same occasion the mothers in question underwent ritual purification.

Being generally familiar with the religious laws and customs of Israel, Mary and Joseph would have known the historical background to the rite of presentation. Essentially it was a ransoming ceremony whereby the liberation of the Jewish people from bondage in Egypt was commemmorated. At the same time the presentation symbolized not only the spiritual deliverance of Israel from the slavery of sin but also its new-found commitment to God. The ransom-price paid by the parents (in this case, two young pigeons) was a token offering in thanksgiving for the divine deliverance.

The truly profound mystery underlying the Infant Saviour's presentation is that he himself was the price to be paid to the Father for mankind's ransom from sin and everlasting death. Besides, he is the one in whom we belong totally to God thanks to our being his brothers and sisters through grace. Thus Jesus, over and above fulfilling the Old Testament rite, enhances it to a transcendent level.

And he does so because, far from being in need of redeeming grace himself, he is its very Author and Giver.

## Two Significant Visitors

But there was yet to be a surprise divine intervention before the Holy Family started on their way back to Bethlehem. Scripture tells us (Lk 2: 25-39) that a venerable old patriarch, Simeon by name, was inspired by the Holy Spirit to approach the parents as they prepared to leave. In his wonderful canticle the old man confessed his belief that the Child he held in his arms was Israel's long-awaited Messianic Saviour; he would bring glory to God's chosen people and the light of revelation to the Gentile world.

Then Simeon's eyes, being illumined with the light of prophecy, saw far into time future when this helpless little Infant would become the Christ of Good Friday—the Man of Sorrows on whose account many in Israel would either rise or fall. Furthermore, this Child would be associated with the sign of the cross, which would be fervently accepted or fiercely rejected in the centuries to come.

Next, Simeon's prophetic gaze focused on the young mother, who along with Joseph was lost in wonderment at what she was hearing. Now the old man saw her as the Mother of Sorrows whose heart would be pierced by the sword of anguish and compassion during the dark hours of the Passion.

St Bernard has written eloquently about this episode.[4] Christ, he says, is in person the Ransom sent by the Father, to whom he would one day be offered not in the temple, nor in Mary's arms, but "between the arms of the cross." And the human race would be ransomed not by the blood of sacrificial pigeons but by the Ransomer's own precious blood.

Finally another Old Testament character—the aged Anna— was led by the Holy Spirit to approach the Holy Family. Like Simeon, she bore witness to the living fulfilment and embodiment of Israel's Messianic prophecies cradled in the arms of his mother.

Joseph listened with intense interest to all these amazing predictions about the Child committed to his fatherly care. On the one hand, the prophetic confirmation of Jesus's status as the world's

Redeemer filled him with awe. On the other hand, he was filled with grief and compassion over what lay ahead for the two treasures in his charge, destined as they were to be respectively the Man and the Mother of Sorrows. Indeed, from that moment on, through his deep and sensitive relationship with his spouse, he shared in advance, and in union with her, something of the pain that would be inflicted by the sword of sorrow.

## A True Fairy Story

To return now with the Holy Family from the temple in Jerusalem to the Nativity scene in Bethlehem. Chesterton suggested that it is the only fairy story which happens to be true. Certainly all the stock ingredients are present in the Bethlehem scenario. To begin with, there is the beautiful and radiant princess of divine grace, now a proud young mother aglow with happiness. In her arms lies the new-born Emmanuel, winning all hearts and stealing the show, as babies unfailingly do. Standing watchfully in the background is the heroic figure of their faithful guardian, while angels fill the night with melodies of adoration and rejoicing.

But every fairy story worthy of the name requires a further key ingredient in the shape of someone or something that is sinister, evil and threatening, an ogre breathing out destruction and death. King Herod of Judea was all this and more. We learn from the gospel how he came into the picture through the magi, who had innocently inquired of him regarding the whereabouts of the new-born King.

We know the sequel. In accordance with God's plan those earnest pilgrims followed their star and, having found the Royal Child, honoured him with their adoration and presented him with gifts. Finally they were instructed from on high to steer clear of Herod when they set off on their homeward journey.

The infamous tyrant's rage over being foiled made him all the more determined to liquidate this infant upstart and would-be king. He instigated the so-called Massacre of the Innocents; all male children up to the age of two in Bethlehem and environs were to be put to the sword.

## Sojourn in Egypt

This spelt imminent danger, of course, for the Christ-Child, and divine providence immediately alerted Joseph to the critical situation. In a dream he was ordered by an angel to take the Child and its mother without the least delay and flee to Egypt.

We can imagine the tension and terror that gripped the hearts of Joseph and Mary as they made hurried preparations to set off into the night. Meanwhile Herod's soldiers and secret police were already preparing to throw a cordon around the Bethlehem area and so cut off all attempts at escape. So there was not a minute to lose.

Joseph, resolute man of action that he was, quickly collected their few possessions, including the gifts presented by the magi, one of which — the gold — would now providentially serve to meet at least some of the expenses lying ahead in their unknown future. Finally, having saddled the animal that would serve as mount for Mary and the tiny, helpless little bundle of humanity that was Emmanuel, the saint hurriedly led them off into the night.

It is commonly assumed that the Holy Family would have headed for Gaza and then followed the coastal road as they slowly made their way down to the Nile delta. What added to the discomforts of the journey, which would have taken them several weeks, was the heat, the glare and the all-pervading dust from the desert terrain.

We do not know with any certainty where the Holy Family took up their abode in Egypt. An old tradition mentions Heliopolis. As for the hypothesis that Cairo is where they settled, it has been supported by 27 apparitions of the Virgin Mary (sometimes with the Infant Jesus in her arms and once accompanied by St Joseph) in 1968 above a church in the Cairo suburb of Zeitoun. Witnessed by hundreds of thousands of people, most of them Muslims, and accompanied by numerous miracles of healing, these apparitions were authenticated by the Coptic authorities. Likewise endorsed by them were the more recent apparitions by the Mother of God above a church in Assiout, which lies to the south of Cairo.

During their sojourn in Egypt, St Joseph would have plied his trade as a carpenter in order to support his wife and Child. As to how long their exile lasted, again we can only conjecture; it could have been anything up to five or six years.

When Herod died, Joseph duly received a message to that effect from an angel in a dream. But on learning that the cruel Archelaus had succeeded his father Herod as ruler of Judea, Joseph decided that the Child's future would be safer in Galilee; accordingly the Holy Family took up their abode in Nazareth.

## REFERENCES FOR CHAPTER THREE
## THE EARLY YEARS

1...John Paul II: Redemptoris Custos, 8
2...Origen: Hom. XI in Luc. 6
3...John Paul II: op. cit. 9
4...St Bernard: Sermon on Purification, 9, 648b

CHAPTER FOUR

# HEAD OF THE HOLY FAMILY

A s an old liturgical prayer proudly proclaims,[1] nowhere in the whole wide world has the sun ever shone on anything more special and distinguished than the holy house of Nazareth. For that humble abode tucked away in an obscure corner of Galilee was the dwelling-place, over the best part of his lifetime, for the Word Incarnate, Emmanuel in person, along with his mother and father.

This was the house wherein Mary and Joseph started to rebuild their lives on returning from exile in Egypt. How happy they must have been to be safely back once more among their own people and settled in their own home. What is more, they now had the added joy of being a little family—indeed, the Holy Family—having received from the Almighty, as the fruit of their virginal union, the golden gift of a Son to share their lives and their home.

How old was the Child, we may wonder, by the time they returned from Egypt? Though no reliable records are available, we may reasonably conjecture that Jesus was by now at least beyond his toddler years. And he was surely a beautiful and winsome youngster, the pride and delight of his devoted parents who, in every sense of the word, adored him. For he was the divine Messiah sent by the Father. And, awesome though it was for Mary and Joseph to contemplate, they were invested with all the responsibilities and rights of parenthood in his regard, their duty being to rear him as a citizen of the very world he had created and was preparing to redeem.

### The Nazareth Scene

Presently we shall be seeing something of the tender interpersonal relationships within the Holy Family and the everyday domestic routines in their lives. But let us first look briefly at the wider picture of Nazareth in their day, the better to understand the general background against which their lives were set.

The first thing to be said about Nazareth is that it was and remains surrounded by much natural beauty. Its white-washed, flat-roofed houses nestled in a wide valley sheltered beneath surrounding hills — gentle, rounded, grassy hills profuse with heather and a colourful variety of wild flowers. Trees, too, are everywhere to be seen on the landscape, as Joseph the carpenter would particularly have appreciated. What also catch the eye are the numerous orchards and vineyards scattered around.

The rich vegetation, the colour and the beauty of this part of Galilee contrast vividly with the harsh, austere features of Judea to the south. Up here the climate is mild, and fresh breezes blow off the Mediterranean not many miles to the west. To the north one sees the towering heights of Mount Tabor where Jesus would one day be transfigured. And quite close by to the east lies the fish-rich Sea of Galilee; it is really an inland lake, dotted around whose shoreline were towns like Bethsaida, Caphernaum and Magdala, all destined to be immortalised in the pages of the gospel.

Because Nazareth was situated near the main trade-routes, it was by no means isolated from the outside world. And, as did Galilee generally, it was blessed with a measure of prosperity, thanks largely to the thriving fish industry and the material benefits plus security afforded by Roman occupation. All in all, then, the Holy Family would likely have enjoyed a modest standard of living free from anything like extreme poverty or want. As for tradesmen like Joseph, there was plenty of work on offer in the entire neighbourhood, notably in nearby Sephoris, the thriving chief town within that area. Herod Antipas had rebuilt it after its destruction by Varus, and it was now the largest and wealthiest centre in the province, spreading its prosperity far and wide.

For Christians, of course, the altogether unique reason for Nazareth's appeal is that it has been sanctified for ever by Jesus and his parents. Almost certainly the same well where Mary used to draw water; the grassy slopes over which the boy Jesus would have roamed; the unchanging silhouette of the surrounding hills that his eyes would so often have traced against the horizon; the setting sun splashing the western sky with a riot of gorgeous colours — images such as these tend to evoke in the pilgrim powerful and nostalgic sentiments centred on the Holy Family.

As Lord Beaverbrook, the press baron, has testified, [2] "a breath of faith and purity seems to flow from that nature which surrounds the youth of Our Lord." So it is not surprising that even a hardened modern-day sceptic like Malcolm Muggeridge was moved largely by his Nazareth impressions to find faith in the great truths of the Christian gospel.

### St Joseph's Fatherhood

The carpenter of Nazareth was head of the Holy Family through his legal fatherhood of the Child born of his lawful wife. However, it is misleading to think of St Joseph as merely the equivalent of an adoptive or foster father. For their Offspring had not been generated by some other male, as that title implies, but was the fruit, albeit miraculous, of his own virginal marriage to the Virgin Mary.

Still less should Joseph be regarded as the equivalent of Our Lord's stepfather—a title that hardly reflects favourably on Mary's honour. Sometimes the saint's fatherhood is referred to as putative or supposed, and this by reason of the common assumption among his contemporaries that he was the Child's natural father (cf. Lk 3: 23). Taken on its own, however, this title conveys nothing of the intimately close and tender father-and-son relationship that linked Joseph with the Divine Person under his guardianship. This relationship has been described accurately and eloquently by Bossuet:[3]

> **"The same divine hand which fashions each man's heart gave a father's heart to Joseph and a son's heart to Jesus, so that Jesus obeyed Joseph and Joseph did not fear to command Jesus. It was because Christ's true Father had chosen Joseph to act as father to his son in this world. And in so doing God had, as it were, charged Joseph's breast with some ray or spark of his own boundless love for his Son. It was this that aroused a father's love in Joseph; so much so that, feeling a father's heart burn within him, Joseph also felt that God was telling him to use a father's authority."**

## Joseph's Exercise of Fatherhood

Likewise by virtue of his marriage bond with Mary, Joseph merits to be called the Divine Child's parent. As St Augustine[4] explains, "Joseph was a parent in the same way that he was the mother's spouse, that is, in mind but not in the flesh."

Having been privileged with Mary to be the first to hold "the Infinite made Infant" in his arms on Christmas night, he subsequently watched him develop through toddlerhood, adolescence, and young manhood—all of which stages of human life, St Irenaeus notes, were sanctified and redeemed by the Son of God's having passed through them himself.

Joseph's responsibility from the very start was to guard, guide and provide for his cherished spouse and the Fruit of their virginal marriage. Food, clothing, shelter, security—these were the primary needs. Clearly, then, Joseph's role as family breadwinner was from a practical point of view the paramount one.

All these duties he discharged not only diligently but with great love and devotion. "By a special gift from heaven," Pius XII wrote,[5] "Joseph showed Jesus all the natural love, all the affectionate solicitude, that a father's heart can know." This was particularly evident in Jesus's infancy and toddler days, as St Leonard of Port-Maurice, among others, has described:[6]

> **"How many times the arms of St Joseph served as a cradle for the Child Jesus! What tender kisses he lavished upon him! And how often he fed him, dressed him, taught him how to speak and to walk!"**

## Jesus's Upbringing

Being truly human, the Word Incarnate lacked what is called experiential knowledge and was therefore subject, like any other child, to the processes of learning, beginning with the very basics. Again like any other child, he grew up at his mother's side. So it would have been principally from her that he learned to lisp his first baby words and to recite his first prayers. And as he grew bigger and his mind started to mature, she would have answered his many questions and taught him how to perform little household chores.

It was customary in Jewish society for male children to remain largely in their mother's care until the age of five, though fathers, too, obviously made a certain contribution. But it wasn't till after that age that they became more actively involved in the upbringing process, with particular reference to the general education of their charges.

Religious and cultural education were closely interwoven in Jewish society, and fathers were most conscientious in playing their part as teachers and instructors. So Joseph would have introduced his Son early on to the psalms and other inspired books of the Old Law, including the great prophecies bearing directly on himself as the Messiah. And, besides teaching him to read the sacred scrolls, he would have taken Jesus to the local synagogue every Sabbath. What also featured importantly in the learning programme was a sound knowledge of Israel's proud history and customs.

### Lessons at Home and at School

As for the broader education that Joseph sought to impart, it included a wide variety of things. The social graces and the accepted rules of private and public behaviour featured prominently among them. So, too, did the world of nature. Very likely the Holy Family would have had their own patch of land on the outskirts of the village, where the young Messiah learned from his guardian such things as how to till soil and grow vegetables. And all around in the surrounding countryside nature offered abundant material from which he would in later years draw homely lessons and parables — things like wheat ripening in the sun, flowers blooming in the fields, and birds building their nests. With regard to vocational knowledge, the Divine Child learned from his father how to use tools like the saw, the chisel and the plane, and thus progressively acquired the basic skills of carpentry.

So it was as the Son of God's primary educator that Joseph performed a task essential to his office as guardian. St Francis of Sales[7] presents him in this connection with a glowing compliment:

> "If princes of this world are most careful in choosing
> tutors for their sons, taking pains to secure the best
> that can be found, do you think that God did not select
> the man who was the most perfectly qualified to be the
> guardian of his eternal Son, the Lord of heaven and
> earth?"

In addition to the solid grounding he gave Jesus in what is nowadays called home-schooling, St Joseph complied with Jewish practice by ensuring his Son's attendance at the village school; customarily this applied to children between the ages of seven and 13. Village schools were usually conducted by the sacristan of the synagogue. And the curriculum was extremely comprehensive, comprising mainly religion, history and literature but also giving pupils a good grounding in reading, writing and arithmetic. Thus the overall intended effect of his school years on the adolescent Messiah was to complement and develop in him the lessons he imbibed from his father and guardian.

## Visit to the Jerusalem Temple

On reaching his twelfth year, Jesus officially came of age. And this now legally obliged him to make the annual pilgrimage to Jerusalem for the feast of the Passover. This he would have done along with his parents, relatives, and a number of fellow-villagers. Invariably the men and women travelled in separate groups, children being free to join either of these.

Passover was the oldest of the three main festivals celebrated annually in Palestine. Always occurring in the spring, its main purpose was to commemorate with solemn liturgy the deliverance of the Israelites from Egyptian bondage. The Passover ceremonial was centred on the temple of Jerusalem, that great sanctuary of Jewish faith and piety. Hence the capital city was swollen over this period with pilgrims from all parts of the homeland as well as overseas. The core item in the liturgical proceedings was the sacrifice and eating of the Paschal lambs which, in accordance with a strict rule, could be slain only in the temple precincts.

We can be sure that St Joseph would have carefully explained to Jesus the rich historical background and symbolic significance surrounding the Passover feast. Doubtless, too, he would have pointed out to him the main features of the magnificent temple built by Herod Antipas.

### Jesus Lost and Found

The source for this episode related by St Luke was almost certainly Mary herself (cf. Lk 2: 41-52). After the first day of the homeward journey, she and Joseph, each having assumed in the meantime that Jesus was with the other group, now discovered that he was with neither. Naturally they were anxious and fearful, the more so as they had never forgotten Herod's murderous bid to liquidate their new-born Son and their emergency escape at dead of night. What now also preyed on their minds was Simeon's dire prophecy about the sword of sorrow poised to pierce Mary's heart because of her Son.

Without delay the anguished parents hastened back to Jerusalem and began searching high and low for the Child, continuing to do so for the next three days. With every passing hour their worst fears increasingly haunted their minds. Indeed, words cannot describe how Our Lady must have felt. As for St Joseph, we are informed by the Venerable Mary of Agreda[8] that he suffered "incomparable affliction and grief and could neither eat nor sleep." Yet throughout this ordeal the sorrowing parents remained in unbroken union with God, begging him not only to help them find their beloved Child but to forgive any possible negligence or failure on their part that might have occasioned this crisis in the first place.

Then at long last, and to their vast relief and overwhelming joy, the distraught parents found the missing Jesus; he was in the temple, astounding those who taught there with his wisdom and the depth of his questions. Thereupon his mother gently—and, in the circumstances, understandably—chided the Boy Jesus for his inexplicable behaviour; to which he made a cryptic reply that was "beyond their understanding." St Luke's account condenses this dialogue admirably:

"My Son, why hast thou treated us so? Think what anguish of mind thy father and I have endured searching for thee. But he asked them, What reason had you to search for me?

Could you not tell that I must needs be in the place which belongs to my Father?" (vv. 48-49)

What lessons, we must ask ourselves, were Our Lord's words meant to convey not only to his puzzled parents but to his future disciples down the centuries? In the first place, he was affirming not only his Messianic status but his perfect conformity to the Father's will. And, secondly, he was endorsing the sacred character of the Jerusalem temple as his Father's sanctuary and shrine.

Just as the transfiguration would be a flashpoint in Christ's public life, giving us a brief glimpse of his divinity, so does this one-off recorded episode in the hidden years point in that same direction. St Luke effectively draws the veil once again over those years when he tells us that Jesus accompanied his parents on the homeward journey and thereafter submitted fully to their authority.

### Plain, Ordinary Folk

"God must love plain, ordinary folk very much," Abraham Lincoln is credited with saying, "seeing he has made so many of them." The secret of Nazareth is that the God-Man who dwelt there not only loved his all-too-plain and ordinary fellow-Nazarenes very much but identified so closely with them and their lifestyle that his divine nature remained completely veiled. Only Mary and Joseph were aware of the awesome truth that Jesus was in fact the Son of the Eternal Father, the Messianic Redeemer come to share our human condition.

As for the human condition in Nazareth, it mirrored in many ways that of the vast majority of people down the ages the world over. Life was largely a matter of the selfsame daily routines with very few highlights or heroics. In other words, life was mostly uneventful, monotonous and repetitive, one day being practically a photocopy of the preceding.

Work, meals, sleep and, above all, prayer—these dominated the landscape of life in the Holy Family's home. Joseph plied his trade in his workshop, while Mary busied herself with household duties and caring for the family's needs. Their Son spent much of his time as he grew older as an apprentice at the workbench with Joseph. By accepting the treadmill of dull daily routine, this blessed trio put a halo round the humdrum and the home alike.

What they particularly looked forward to each week was the Sabbath—the day of rest, reflection and prayer. Heralded by a trumpet-blast on Friday evening, it lasted till sundown on Saturday. Very faithfully Jesus, Mary and Joseph would join the congregation in the synagogue for prayers and Scripture readings.

## The Holy Family

By being born and reared in a family setting, the Word-made-Flesh consecrated marriage and family values generally. Thanks to this consecration the Holy Family became, under "its lord and master" St Joseph, the prototype and shining exemplar for all Christian families in the centuries ahead. The lofty ideal set for their imitation by the inspiring Nazareth model, says Paul VI,[9] is that Christian homes become in their turn "sanctuaries of love and cradles of life."

"A sanctuary of love"—the Holy Family was such to a supreme degree. The spousal love between Joseph and Mary grew ever purer and stronger through their ardent faith and shared parental love for the Divine Child whom they cherished beyond words. An old Japanese proverb here comes to mind: "A father's love is higher than any mountain, while a mother's is more than ocean-deep."

As for their Child's filial love towards Mary and Joseph, its strength and purity flowed from a human nature unblemished by sin and overflowing with divine grace. And this love was expressed in the humble, prompt way he showed them respect and obedience.

## Lessons from the Holy Family

In referring to the Nazareth Family as "a cradle of life," Paul VI had in mind the entire gamut of values and virtues the Christian faith associates with human love and sexuality. In this domain Joseph and Mary act as role-models for Christian chastity both inside and outside the married state.

Today's so-called culture of death is the product of the unchaste environment that endangers Christian chastity at every level; it finds expression in sinful practices such as pre-marital sex, contraception, marital infidelity, homosexuality, same-sex marriage and—surely vilest and sinfullest of all—abortion.

What the culture of death has also indirectly brought about is a marked increase in the number of dysfunctional marriages, broken homes and fatherless families. A distinguished American leader, Archbishop Charles Chaput, warmly recommends the head of the Holy Family of Nazareth as a special patron in our campaign to restore dignity and sanctity to families and homes. His text reads:[10]

**"Joseph was a living witness to the nobility of human labour and the dignity of married life. If we hope to restore the identity of fathers in our families and in our culture, if we hope to rebuild the integrity of family life in our communities, we should look first to Joseph. We have no better model."**

## REFERENCES FOR CHAPTER FOUR
## THE HOLY FAMILY

1...Feast of the Holy Family: Hymn
2...Lord Beaverbrook: The Divine Propagandist, 42, 43
3...Jacques Bossuet: Oeuvres Completes: Sermon on St Joseph
4...St Augustine: De Consensu Evangelii, 2,1
5...Pius X11: Radio Address, 19 February 1958
6...St Leonard of Port-Maurice: "The Glories of Joseph," p 169
7...St Francis of Sales: Discourse 19 in Complete Works of St
    Francis of Sales, VI
8...Ven. Mary of Agreda: Mystical City of God
9...Paul V1: Address to Equipes Notre Dame, 4 May 1970
10.Archishop Charles Chaput: quoted in "Voices," Winter 2000

CHAPTER FIVE

# JOSEPH THE WORKER

O f all St Joseph's titles, this is one of the best-known and most popular. For it highlights what in material terms was clearly the saint's major contribution to the Redeemer's mission: namely, his role as breadwinner for the Holy Family through his work as a carpenter.

But this particular title serves at the same time to open a window on the world of work as such, inviting us to examine the significance of work in itself and, more importantly, in God's creative and redemptive plan for mankind. In which plan every single one of us is involved in some way and to some degree, since we are all born subject to the law of work understood in its broadest sense. In this perspective, then, the entire human race may be said to constitute the "workers of the world." But in applying Karl Marx's label we need to emphasize that all human work, howsoever humble and menial, is dignified and never demeaning. Nor should the label be misapplied, Marxist-fashion, as an engine of envy and class-warfare.

## God's Hands in Nazareth

We shall presently be looking at these and other considerations implicit in Joseph's title as worker. But first let us reflect upon and relish an amazing truth that shines out from his Nazareth workshop like a beacon. Leo XIII[1] was lost in sheer wonderment at it. For what this truth reveals is that in an obscure Galilean village, working alongside Joseph and under his direction, day in and day out over a good many years, and remaining all the while completely unnoticed by the world, "the very hands of God in person wielded the tools of a carpenter."

Besides being amazing, this revelation bristles with paradoxes.

For it proclaims that the Almighty Being who, at a mere command of his will, created this vast and mysterious universe out of nothing, became, as the Word-made-flesh, a carpenter, handling and shaping the very wood and other materials he himself had called into existence by his creative power.

## The Creator-Carpenter

This paradox of the all-powerful Creator humbly practising the trade of carpentry was not lost on the great minds of the early Christian centuries. One and all they praised and thanked God for that sublime mystery which made the paradox possible in the first place: the Incarnation of the Second Person as Son of the carpenter of Nazareth. And those same great minds went on to honour that carpenter as the key-man whose calling determined that Emmanuel should follow in his footsteps and duly taught him the ABC of the trade. In St Ephrem's words, "it was the hands of Joseph the carpenter that trained and guided the hands of God."

Nor was this Creator-become-carpenter paradox lost on that privileged man whose hands trained and guided the divine ones. Constantly St Joseph would have reflected on the stunning reality that young Emmanuel working alongside him and under his tutelage was, in person, albeit clothed in human nature, Almighty Yahweh himself, the Divine Author of the universe, the King of the Ages before whom the psalmist bids us bow down in adoration: "It was thou, Lord, that didst lay the foundations of earth when time began; it was thy hand that built the heavens" (Ps 101: 26).

Interestingly enough, the "hand that built the heavens" is apt to display its artistry most strikingly in the brilliant night-sky so often to be seen over Galilee. We can well imagine the Holy Family relaxing on their flat roof-top in the cool of evening and admiring the sheer loveliness of the starlit heavens spread out above them like a canopy. And their sentiments would instinctively have echoed the psalmist's:

**"I look up at those heavens of thine, the work of thy hands, at the moon and the stars, which thou hast set in**

**their places....See how the skies proclaim God's glory,
how the vault of heaven betrays his craftsmanship" (Ps
8:4; 18: 1)**

Yes, incredible though it may seem, the Craftsman whose
handiwork is written all over the night-skies became a member of
the human race, learnt his craft from the man he called "father,"
and prepared thereby to earn his own living. St Joseph, for his part,
would doubtless have cherished with special fondness his early
memories of the Child Jesus learning his first elementary lessons
in the workshop. Ronald Knox's poem on St Joseph delicately
captures those moments:

**"And surely 'twas a gracious thing
When, standing at his father's knee,
The world's great Craftsman and its King
Not king but craftsman learned to be."**

### Visiting St Joseph's Workshop

At the age of 12, Jewish boys officially became not only "sons of the
law" but "sons of work," thereupon beginning their apprenticeship
in the occupation traditionally practised by the father. Every male
was strictly bound by this custom, even the great rabbi Hillel having trained as a wood-cutter. And we know that St Paul, like his
converts Aquila and Piscilla, formerly earned his living as a tent-
maker (cf. Acts 18: 3).

Thus it was that, under Joseph's guidance and direct authority,
Jesus progressively acquired the skills of a carpenter and general
handyman (which is what the Greek word *tekton* means). Timber
was available in abundance throughout Galilee, and Joseph would
have taught his son to identify the different species of tree—fir,
oak, poplar, sycamore, mulberry, cedar, cypress, etcetera—and
learn their respective qualities in relation to carpentry and its uses.
Wood-cutters supplied the trade's basic raw material: tree-logs,
which were then trimmed and shaped into the intended end-prod-
uct.

Another rudimentary lesson Joseph would have taught his able and willing Apprentice was the use of the various tools and instruments essential to their craft. Chief among these were the axe, saw, hammer, mallet, nails, chisel and plane.

As in every village workshop of its kind, this father-and-Son team made new things and repaired damaged ones; these ranged from domestic furniture and fittings to agricultural and farming implements and materials. Hence Joseph and his Assistant dealt with a wide-ranging selection of articles; these included doors, window-shutters, tables, stools, lampstands, kneading troughs, pots, jars, basins, looms, spindles, ploughs, harness poles, goads and yokes for oxen, and so on.

There could hardly ever have been a shortage of work. For trained carpenters were frequently hired also by clients in neighbouring towns and villages. Besides, over that general period Galilee was experiencing something of a boom; this had been triggered off by the lavish building programme initiated by Herod and now being continued by his son. The programme included the wholesale development of Sephoris, the former Galilean capital, situated just over the crest of a hill near Nazareth. Even nearer lay Japhia, a flourishing new settlement offering ample job-opportunities for local craftsmen and handymen.

## The Third Nazareth Worker

An abiding consolation and joy for Jesus and Joseph midst their daily toil was that Mary, the devoted mother and spouse, was ever at their service in the background. She was the loving heart of their home, lavishing her attentions on the two men whose lives she shared so intimately, and thereby creating for them the optimum domestic environment wherein to ply their trade and earn a steady livelihood. In her own way, therefore, Mary was the indispensable third worker in the Holy Family—the earthly trinity which mirrored the heavenly one.

So we cannot really omit to look briefly at the essential duties and services "Mary the Worker" would have rendered her menfolk over those hidden years in Nazareth. She swept the house and kept it clean and orderly. She washed the family's clothing. Having ground the corn and wheat, she kneaded and baked the bread. She drew water from the public well, carrying her waterpot on her head. She milked the goat. She tended the vegetable patch and purchased provisions such as oil, fish, cheese, fruit, honey and wine. She cooked and prepared the meals (the principal one being at sundown). She spun wool and flax, and with these wove the materials for the family's garments, which she would also mend as occasion required.

In a thousand-and-one ways, then, Our Lady merited her proud title as the third worker of Nazareth. And in the process she added a new dignity and sanctification to the often taken-for-granted work of housewives in every age the world over.

## The Gospel of Work

During his visit to Nazareth in 1964, Paul VI stressed that what we learn from this hallowed place, besides much else, is "a lesson of work." John Paul II later amplified this expression to "a gospel of work." [2] And what this particular gospel proclaims is that all human work has been dignified and sanctified beyond measure by the Son of God who, in sharing Joseph's daily toil, "truly worked with human hands." [3]

The "gospel of work" further endorses that man is by his very nature *homo faber;* he needs work of one kind or another not simply to make a living but as a form of self-expression and self-fulfilment. It has been calculated that over 30 passages in the Old Testament (and more than 100 in the Talmud) stress not only work's nobility but its necessity. These sources were equally well aware that sound psychological health, let alone hard economic factors, demand that a man does some kind of work. Moral issues likewise enter the equation; idleness, laziness and sloth are offensive to God besides being corrosive of character and moral integrity.

But the really prize lesson of the gospel issuing from St Joseph's workshop is that, in John Paul II's words,[4] "work has been taken up into the mystery of the Incarnation and so has been redeemed in a special way." This transforming effect applies to work of every conceivable kind, whether it be mental or manual, "of the head or

**47**

of the hands."

Nazareth teaches us that man is called to prolong and develop the work of creation by subduing the earth (cf. Gen. 1: 28); thus it falls to him as a duty. "If anyone will not work," runs the familiar text, "let him not eat" (2 Thess. 3: 10). And because work in our world under the penalties of original sin can entail a degree of sweat and hardship (cf. Gen. 3: 14- 19), it becomes not only redemptive if offered in union with the Nazareth Carpenter but participates co-redemptively in his saving mission.[5]

## Your Workplace is Holy Ground

Another secret we learn from St Joseph's workplace, to quote John Paul II once again,[6] is that work was there regarded by Jesus and his parents "not merely as a means of earning a living but as a daily expression of love." That is to say, their work was lovingly accepted in the first place as a basic law of human life as planned by the Creator. Secondly, for Mary and Joseph it became sanctifying and redemptive through being united in spirit with the Redeemer's work and co-offered with his to the Eternal Father.

As has been noted, this golden effect applies to each and every kind of employment without exception. Whatever a man's profession, calling, occupation or trade, his work, whether he realises it or not, has been hallowed and blessed by the divine Artisan who learned his trade from Joseph. So, by uniting themselves with that Artisan, people in every walk of life enjoy the privilege of doing their work, as he did his, in God, with God, and for God.

It follows that a man's workplace, no matter of what kind it may be, becomes holy ground by reason of its potential linkage with its Nazareth counterpart. Be it factory floor, business office, farmyard, building site, hospital ward, schoolroom, shipyard, kitchen, boardroom, coal mine, or anything else, every human workplace becomes to the eyes of faith a living shrine of the Holy Spirit. And it does so as a direct benefit from the humble Galilean workplace wherein "the hands of Joseph the carpenter trained and guided the hands of God."

## Blessed are the Lowly

John Paul II has observed that in the Nazareth-inspired gospel of work a special prominence is accorded to "manual labour." And with good reason, too, seeing that the vast majority of Christ's followers have traditionally been working-class folk earning their living by manual toil.

One thinks here of Blessed Matt Talbot, the Dublin workman who spent a lifetime as a labourer on building-sites; he would offer his daily work, in union with St Joseph, to the Divine Workman, of whom he once remarked in his laconic way, "Christ the Carpenter must have a close interest in those who work."

One also thinks here of Blessed Charles de Foucauld; wishing to share St Joseph's lowly status as a manual worker, he prevailed upon the Poor Clares, during his sojourn in Nazareth, to allot him the task of sweeping their convent floors.

Examples abound of Christian zeal in offering to God work of every kind in the spirit of penance and prayer. St Benedict was imbued with this principle, as is seen in his famous motto: "To work is to pray." Similarly St Bernadette; on becoming an invalid she famously declared that this was the new-found employment she could and would offer to God.

Gerard Manley Hopkins had a sharp insight into how the humblest tasks, howsoever low-grade they may be socially and economically, can glorify God and sanctify the worker:[7]

**"It is not only prayer that gives glory to God but work.
Smiting on an anvil, sowing a beam, whitewashing a wall,
Driving horses, reaping, scouring—everything gives God
Glory. To lift up hands in prayer gives God glory.
But a man with a dung-fork in his hand,
Or a woman with a slop-pail,
They give God glory too."**

## Lifeworks in Nazareth

Earlier we saw something of the kind of work that filled the days of the Holy Family of Nazareth. But their various tasks, sanctifying though they were, formed but a part of the larger work-plan designed for each of them by the God of providence. This work-plan was in effect the specific lifework assigned them by the Eternal Father. And the safe and sure guideline he provided for the fulfilment of this lifework lay in their adherence to his holy will. The psalmist's words would have served ideally as a motto for their humble home:

**"To do thy will, O my God, is all my desire; to carry out that law of thine which is written in my heart." [Ps 39: 9].**

We know what the lifework of Jesus was. We also know from the gospels that, from start to finish, it was a masterpiece of perfect conformity in all things and at all times to his Father's will. Accordingly the Son of God would come into this world as its Incarnate Redeemer and offer his life for the salvation of the human race. For his God-given goal, his underlying mission, his burning desire throughout his earthly days was to be humanity's Victim-Saviour. This prompted Chesterton to remark that Christ is the only man ever to come into this world with the express purpose of dying. And his deathwork set the seal on his lifework. Hence he could say at the end, "Consummatum est." For his lifework as planned by the Father had been accomplished.

We also know what Mary's lifework was and that it was no less a masterpiece of perfect conformity to the Father's will. Essentially her role was to be not only the Redeemer's mother but, in a subordinate and secondary capacity, the Co-redemptrix of all the graces he won for us. This honorable role was merited by Mary through her close and lifelong union with the Redeemer, reaching its climax when she co-offered with him her own maternal anguish and sorrow while his great act of redemption was being accomplished in the agony of Good Friday.

As for St Joseph's lifework, it is summed up by the Church when it describes him as "the just and obedient man who helped to carry out the great mysteries of our salvation."[8]. He rendered that help in his capacity as the Holy Family's guardian, provider and head. And, in carrying out these duties, he made it humanly possible for "his two treasures" each to accomplish the lifework required of them by the Father. In a word, St Joseph's whole lifework was to serve and support theirs. This explains why, apart from Mary's, no human lifework could possibly be higher or holier than that of her spouse.

## Our Personal Lifework

As with the illustrious Nazareth trio, every single human person has been entrusted by the Creator with a special lifework—one made and measured for each of us personally so that we might give him maximum glory and service. John Paul II's maxim emphasizes this principle. "Everyone," it says, "has a special something to do for God."

Again as with the Holy Family, the general guideline we are to follow in performing our lifework is to be found in doing the divine will at all times. What Christ said of himself in this matter should become the lodestar of our lives: "My meat is to do the will of him who sent me, and to accomplish the task he gave me" [Jn 4:34].

But can it be said that each of us has been "sent" by God? The answer is Yes. God's gift of a lifetime's task to everyone clearly implies that they have received from him a corresponding mission and purpose. And though the precise pattern of that lifework may at times be difficult to discern, it remains ever with us as we make our pilgrim-way down the years. And the whole point of our pilgrimage, as St Ignatius saw so clearly, is that we praise, reverence and serve our Creator and thereby save our souls.

It goes without saying, then, that the perfect fulfilment of God's plan should be our overriding aim in life. And here we can draw much help from the Holy Spirit's gift of wisdom. For its essential benefit is that it gives us a true perspective on life, enabling us to view it not only as a divine gift but as a sacred task committed to us on earth. Only in eternal life will we fully grasp the scope and grandeur of what we have done for our Creator and Redeemer;

also we shall there see how we have helped others—please God, many others—to reach the same glorious destination. Newman saw deeply into all these realities:[9]

> "Each person has a mission. God has created me to do him some special service. He has committed some work to me which he has not committed to another . . . I have my mission—I may never know it in this life, but I shall be told it in the next. I am a link in a chain, a bond of connection between persons. He has not created me for naught. I shall do good. I shall do his work . . . He does nothing in vain. He knows what he is about."

## Joseph and Our Work

The Church reminds us, appropriately enough on the feast of Joseph the Worker, that God has called man "to develop and use his gifts for the good of others." And the saint, who was officially instituted as Patron of Workers by Pius XII, is petitioned in the liturgy to "help us do the work that God has asked."[10]

Besides Pius XII, every single pontiff from Pius IX up till the present incumbent has contributed richly to the "garland of honours" heaped upon the Carpenter of Nazareth, many of their tributes being directed to him as the model and patron of workers.

To give two examples. Pius X recommended us in a well-known prayer to ask Joseph, among other favours, for the grace "to work in a spirit of thanksgiving and joy." And John XXIII, in an equally well-known prayer, makes special mention of the saint's special charism for "transforming work into a means of high sanctification."

As we saw earlier, our workplace, whatever it happens to be, is holy ground. And it becomes holier in the measure that we learn and live the Nazareth workshop's golden lesson: work is a gospel—the gospel of love and service. In Kahlil Gibran's famous line, "work is love made visible."[11] But the last word on this subject is best left to that celebrated tent-maker who, we can be quite sure, would have practised what he preached:

"Whatever your work is, put your heart into it as
if it were for the Lord and not for men . . . It is Christ
the Lord that you are serving" [Col 3: 23-24].

## REFERENCES FOR CHAPTER FIVE
## JOSEPH THE WORKER

1...Leo XIII: Neminem Fugit
2...John Paul II: Laborem Exercens
3...Vatican II: Gaudium et Spes, 22
4...John Paul II: Redemptoris Custos, 22
5...cf. Catechism of the Catholic Church: # 2427
6...John Paul II: ibid.
7...Gerard Manley Hopkins: Collected Poems: "Work"
8...Votive Mass of St Joseph: Post-Communion Prayer
9...Cardinal John Henry Newman: Meditations and Devotions
10..Votive Mass of St Joseph the Worker: Opening Prayer
11..Kahlil Gibran: The Prophet

# St. Joseph, Patron of the Triumph

# CHAPTER SIX

# JOSEPH, MAN OF FAITH

S t Joseph is acclaimed by the Church as "the just and obedient man who helped to carry out the mysteries of our salvation."[1] The word "obedient" here refers to "the obedience of faith" (Rom 1:5). And what this text tells us is that St Joseph gave an instant and unequivocal Yes to everything God had revealed, besides embracing and carrying out the least indication of his will. Indeed, what the Redeemer was later to say of himself could equally be applied in its measure to the guardian of his formative years: "My meat is to do the will of him who sent me and to accomplish the task he gave me" (Jn 4: 34).

So undiluted, in fact, was Joseph's obedience of faith, and so unhesitating and unswerving, that from earliest times it has been recognized as something of a prodigy by a whole galaxy of theologians, saints and mystics. Many of these even pay Joseph the compliment of measuring his faith against Mary's, rating it second only to hers among all God's creatures. So Cardinal Peter d'Ailly of Cambrai was really speaking for all Christian tradition when he apostrophized the saint as follows:[2]

**"O Joseph, most just of men! How could you so promptly and firmly have believed mysteries so novel, so unheard-of, and so profound?"**

## Two Faiths Meet

We shall presently be looking at some of these "novel and unheard-of things" that were to exercise Joseph's faith. But let us first recall St Augustine's key formula for reaching a correct assessment of the Virgin's spouse and his contribution to the Messianic Kingdom. The formula goes: it is through Mary and because of Mary that St Joseph is what he is and does what he does.

This applies in very particular to Joseph's faith, which, besides being focused entirely on serving Mary's maternal mission, drew constant light and support from her own superlative faith. And, like his cherished spouse, he was blessed because he believed that the promises God had made her would be fulfilled (cf. Lk I:45).

Being a true Israelite and therefore a staunch believer, St Joseph gave the assent of faith to everything revealed by Yahweh to the People of Israel and duly enshrined in the sacred books of the Law and the Prophets. Again like every true Israelite, he believed with passionate conviction in the central prophecy that ran like an ever-recurring motif throughout the inspired books.

This prophecy told of a stupendous and exciting truth, for the fulfilment of which a long line of patriarchs, prophets and kings had yearned and prayed. It stated nothing less than that the Son of God, the mighty Creator and Lord of heaven and earth, would come among us in person as Emmanuel, God-with-us, the Word-made-flesh, the Messianic Redeemer of the world.

Joseph's already strong faith was soon due to receive a quantum increase through his personal involvement in the Messianic scenario. He was informed through a private revelation not only that the Messiah's advent was imminent but, wildly impossible though it seemed, he himself, the lowly carpenter of Nazareth, had actually been chosen by providence to play a leading role in the enactment of this sacred event.

Nor was that all. Through the same revelation Joseph's faith took an additional quantum leap forward when he learned—and accepted—that the principal part in the drama was to be played by the woman who was his wedded wife. Virginal though Mary was and would remain, she was nonetheless the mother-elect of the Messianic Saviour; indeed, she had already conceived him in her womb through the power of the Holy Spirit.

## Adventure and Pilgrimage

Before proceeding any further into this rarefied and transcendent faith-world to which Our Lady and St Joseph found themselves elevated, it will be as well if we briefly refresh our memories as to what faith as such essentially means. In general terms, it is the free and undoubting assent we are enabled through God's grace to give to whatever truths he reveals about himself and his designs for our salvation. As for a good working description of faith, it is the on-going adventure of our mind and heart—under the action of grace—into the truths communicated by God.

In this light we can see how Mary's faith and Joseph's became very much of a joint adventure through being focused so personally on the mystery of Emmanuel and their own momentous responsibilities in his regard. In other words, their linked involvement to such a hands-on degree in the drama of Jesus brought their respective faiths together on closely parallel lines.

Pope John Paul II likens their joint adventure into the new world brought by Emmanuel to a co-pilgrimage of faith; it began when the God-Man, though still in his mother's womb, as it were joined his parents' hands and hearts in his love and service. The papal text reads:[3]

**"Joseph was the first to be placed by God on the path of Mary's pilgrimage of faith . . . the first to share in the faith of the mother of God . . . when he accepted as truth coming from God the very thing she had already accepted at the Annunciation."**

### A Virgin Shall Conceive

The first "novel and unheard-of thing" to test Joseph's faith was Mary's virginal conception of the Christ-Child. We can readily understand how perplexed he initially was at his spouse's inexplicable pregnancy. Reasoning that it could only be explained in terms of some high and supernatural design into which Our Lady had been caught up as an instrument, and in which he himself was bound to be a complete outsider and an unworthy one at that, he decided to divorce her privately.

Again we can readily understand how relieving and consoling for the troubled Joseph the angel's prompt intervention proved to be at that critical juncture:

> **"Fear not, Joseph . . . to take thy wife Mary to thyself . . . for it is by the power of the Holy Spirit that she has conceived this child" (Mt 1: 20).**

The point here is that, so high was the calibre of Joseph's faith, he accepted this explanation immediately and without questioning; moreover, he acted upon it straightaway. Abandoning his divorce plan, the man of faith duly went ahead with the all-necessary formality of receiving Mary into his home, thereby setting the definitive seal on their marriage and preparing the way for the future Holy Family.

To get the full measure of what can fairly be described as Joseph's mega-faith, we have only to compare him with Abraham, who is upheld in the Old Testament as the exemplar of perfect faith—a title he earned chiefly for having believed that a sterile woman would bear a child. Joseph, on the other hand, said the Yes of faith to the angelic message that a like miraculous phenomenon had actually and recently befallen someone who was a virgin—indeed, his very own Mary. With the simplicity and directness of a child, the saint, in John Paul II's words,[4] "accepted as truth coming from God the very thing that Mary had already accepted at the Annunciation."

## Another "New and Unheard-of Thing"

Nor was that the only prophesied miracle regarding Mary's motherhood to which Joseph gave his unqualified assent. A further miraculous dimension, one infinitely greater in every respect, was tied in with the virgin's miraculous conception. It was that the Conceived would be of divine origin. The angelic message had made this abundantly clear:

> **"Joseph, son of David . . . it is by the power of the Holy Spirit that she has conceived this child; and she will bear a son, whom thou shalt call Jesus, for he is to save his people from their sins" (Mt I: 21).**

We can be quite sure that Mary knew from what the angel had told her that the Infant in her womb was the eternal Son of God. And this had been confirmed when Elizabeth acclaimed her as "the mother of my Lord" (Lk 1: 43). We can be equally sure that Mary would have informed Joseph about these and other circumstances surrounding her virginal maternity, thus serving to build up his faith still further in the divinity of her unborn Son.

Some commentators have expressed doubt whether Mary and Joseph knew from the outset that the living being cradled in her womb was a Divine Person who had taken a humanity drawn from her own. While Mary and her spouse knew that he was the Messiah, these commentators contend, it was not till a later stage of the Messiah's life that his parents came to realise that their miraculously conceived Offspring was actually the eternal Son of God.

But, as Suarez for one has pointed out, such an interpretation contradicts the whole sense and tradition of the Church, which goes back to the theological giants of the patristic age. Pope St Leo the Great, for example, declared:[5]

**"A royal virgin of the race of David is chosen, who would become pregnant with a sacred fetus and would conceive her divine and human offspring in her mind before doing so in her body"**

The same belief is championed by many doctors of the Church, including Saints Thomas, Alphonsus and Francis off Sales, as well as by a succession of modern popes. Pius XII, for instance,[6] taking up a theme advanced by St Thomas, says that at the Annunciation Our Lady "stood proxy for all mankind and contracted a spiritual marriage between the Son of God and human nature." It stands to reason, then, that she could not have done what she did without knowing that her Son was God.

Clearly the heavenly messenger would seriously have misled Mary and Joseph if he had really meant to announce that her Offspring was human and nothing more. Moreover, why would God wish to be the Father by supernatural conception of a child who was not in actual fact his own Divine Son? Furthermore, this is the only example throughout Scripture where the term "Son of God" is applied to someone due to be conceived through a direct and divine intervention. And later on Christ confirmed this when he showed that "Son of God" referred to his own divine filiation.

## The Eyes of Faith

The mystery and beauty of Christmas have been well expressed in a liturgical prayer: [7]

"In the wonder of the Incarnation your Eternal Word has brought to the eyes of faith a new and radiant vision of your glory. In him we see our God made visible, and so are caught up in the love of the God we cannot see."

Mary and Joseph had the distinction of being the first-ever to see the Christ-Child with their bodily eyes. Similarly they were the first to behold with the eyes of faith the new and radiant vision of God-made-visible, the Word-made-flesh, the Infinite-made-Infant, the Maker of heaven and earth now lying helpless in the manger. Besides, Mary and Joseph were the first to adore the sacred humanity of the new-born Saviour, "in whom the whole fulness of deity dwelt bodily" (Col 2: 9). And their adoration was soon to be followed by that of the Bethlehem shepherds and the Three Wise Men.

A unique privilege Joseph shared with his spouse was that of being, in Leo XIII's words,[8] "the first depositary of the divine mystery." The divine mystery in question was, in fact, twofold, comprising two key elements in God's redemptive plan: the Virginal Conception and the Incarnation.

So Joseph, together with Mary, was the chosen confidant and guardian of what St Paul refers to as "the mystery hidden for ages in God"—the mystery of the Incarnation due to be fulfilled "in the fullness of time when God sent his Son born of a woman" (Eph 3: 9; Gal 4: 4-5).

## Close to the Incarnation

We have seen that Joseph's adventure of faith, like Mary's, was from start to finish ordained towards the mystery of the redemptive Incarnation. For they were the couple chosen to provide the infrastructure, so to call it, for the Eternal Word's entry into our world in an appropriately normal way; this would serve to identify him more closely with his fellow-men not only by having parents but by being reared in a stable family setting.

Herein we see how indispensable was the cooperation of Mary and Joseph in God's redemptive plan for his Son's Incarnation. This signifies the uniting of the Second Person of the Trinity with a humanity drawn from his mother. In other words, Jesus is a divine person with a dual nature, divine and human; he is the God-Man, fully God yet fully Man. St Thomas wrote of this stupendous mystery:

> **"The human mind cannot conceive anything more remarkable than the immense reality contained within it."**

Both through their faith and in actual fact Mary and Joseph welcomed this "immense reality" into their lives, even sharing their home with him for long years. And because their lives were wholly at the service of their Messianic Son, in whom the divine-human union was literally embodied, they themselves were raised by God to a uniquely exalted status and role in his life and mission.

Upon the God-Man's mother, says St Thomas,[10] was conferred "a quasi-infinite dignity." As for St Joseph, it is generally agreed that his ministry in the divine scheme of things exceeded in honour and importance every other ministry, angelic or human, barring that of his spouse. St Basil gives the underlying reason. "Which angel or saint," he asks, "has ever deserved to be called father of the Son of God?"

Previous pages have shown that the defining feature of St Joseph's contribution to God's plan of redemption was his fatherhood of the Redeemer. And, as we would expect, Joseph's faith found in the performance of his paternal duties a wellspring of support, illumination and consolation. Pope Pius XI[11] had a deep insight into how both faith and love operated in the saint's relationship with the Child who called him father:

> "Through Joseph's fatherhood we are in the order of the Incarnation and Redemption established by the personal union of God with man. Joseph was privileged to give to the Word Incarnate over the years love, devotion, protection, instruction, companionship, all of which kept him in close intimacy with Jesus."

## Shadow of the Trinity

Joseph's faith further enabled him to perceive yet another dimension to his ministry within the divine-human mysteries. It was that his fatherly relationship with Jesus became an earthly reflection, howsoever faint and distant, of the First Person's role towards the Second in the life of the Trinity. As St Francis de Sales once put it,[12] "Joseph was the deputy father of Our Lord in lieu of the Eternal Father."

Like every human father, Joseph shared the authority of him "from whom all fatherhood in heaven and on earth takes its title" (Eph 3: 15). But, unlike every other human father, Joseph took from the Heavenly Father the title that dignified him as his earthly representative, vicar, shadow, image.

What Joseph and Mary also beheld with the eyes of faith followed logically from the foregoing: namely, together with Jesus, they formed not simply an ordinary human trio but an earthly trinity in the image and likeness of the heavenly one. Hence Gerson hails the Nazareth family as "the wonderful trinity of Jesus, Mary and Joseph."

This theme has been taken up and developed by many saints and dostors. Francis de Sales, for example, writes:[13] "We may say that the Holy Family was a trinity on earth which in a certain way represented the Blessed Trinity itself." He further points out that the counterpart of the Holy Spirit in the earthly trinity is, of course, she upon whom he descended on that day of days in Nazareth.

St Alphonsus Liguori was similarly devoted to the "earthly trinitarian family," whose head was Joseph, the man of faith, a man, moreover, whose care for Our Lord combined the tenderest fatherly affection with the purest creaturely adoration. In his touching poem dedicated to Christ's earthly father, Alphonsus puts on his lips the following well-known prayer:

> **"Since thou the name of father hast bestowed**
> **On me, my Jesus, let me call thee Son.**
> **My Son, I love, I love thee! Yes, my God,**
> **Forever will I love thee, dearest One!"**

### Joseph's Ladder

A belief that permeates the Old Testament and exerted a major influence in Joseph's life is the existence of an invisible spirit-world of angels and demons. How dramatically this belief found concrete expression at certain crisis-points in the saint's career, even determining the direction and shape of momentous things to come, is found in the New Testament's so-called Infancy Narratives.

"An angel of the Lord appeared to him in a dream" (Mt 1: 20). Thus does the gospel begin its recording of the first angelic apparition experienced by St Joseph. And we know how significant, indeed crucial, was its sequel: his mental anguish over Mary's inexplicable pregnancy was instantly dispelled; his marriage no longer faced the prospect of divorce; and his future destiny as the Messiah's paternal guardian was set firmly on course.

The second recorded instance of angelic activity in Joseph's life was on the night of the Saviour's birth. He and Mary doubtless heard the chorus of angels serenading the new-born King with those first-ever Christmas carols. Which for the Child's wondering parents would surely have been a feast of faith as well as heavenly melody. Doubtless, too, they would have heard the shepherds tell of how it had been angels who directed them to the Nativity scene.

Meanwhile fallen angels were likewise taking an active hand in proceedings by aiding and abetting King Herod's murderous plot to liquidate the new-born King and so remove a potential threat to his throne. Again an angel of God appeared in a dream to the Saviour's guardian, instructing him to flee immediately with mother and Child to Egypt and so escape the imminent massacre.

In God's good time an angel appeared once more in a dream to the exiled Joseph, telling him to return with Mary and Jesus to his homeland. Finally, he was favoured with a fifth recorded dream-vision, the angel directing him to settle in Galilee instead of Judea because of the threat posed by Herod's son.

But by no means were St Joseph's communications with the angelic world limited to these critical episodes early on in his guardianship. Gifted as he was with eyes of faith that enjoyed the keenest vision, he was on familiar terms with everyone and everything within the invisible kingdom of God. Consequently his Nazareth home was transformed through faith into a hallowed sanctuary of the supernatural world, including the angelic hosts forever adoring their Incarnate Creator and reverencing their queen-elect.

So the promise that Christ would later make to Nathanael as reward for his faith had become an everyday reality for St Joseph: "You will see the heavens opened and the angels of God ascending and descending upon the Son of Man" (Jn 1: 51). Similarly, just as the patriarch Jacob saw, pitched between heaven and earth, "a stairway for the angels of God to ascend and descend" (Gen 28: 17), the patriarch of Nazareth beheld daily, with his eagle-eyed faith-vision, the identical mystical ladder linking us with the angels of God.

## Lord, Increase Our Faith

As we have been seeing, St Joseph was richly endowed with what is technically known as the virtue of faith. Being a created reality and therefore finite, this virtue is ever capable of growth, enlargement, development, deepening, improvement, purification—all of which processes find a place in the gospel prayer, "Lord, increase our faith" (Lk 17: 5). Even Mary's faith, which was strong enough to move mountains, grew ever stronger and purer as she advanced on her pilgrimage down the years, seeing daily ever deeper into the divine truths she treasured in her heart (cf. Lk 2: 51).

The same principle of growth applied, of course, to St Joseph's faith. And, as is always the case, this growth took place in two distinct ways. Firstly, he came to see divine truths ever more clearly and sharply defined; that is, his eyes of faith developed an ever-keener vision of supernatural realities. As a result, the virtue of faith, which basically empowers us to believe in God and his kingdom, took on in Joseph an added intensity, an ever-higher voltage.

In the second place, Joseph's faith grew in his grasp or understanding of the supernatural truths contained in the package of revelation as he knew it. In which growth that special gift of the Holy Spirit we know as understanding played a dominant part. Thus the Head of the Holy Family was enabled to penetrate and comprehend ever more lucidly, as well as relish more appreciatively, the mysteries of salvation that daily filled his life so intimately at a domestic level.

It was precisely that level of everyday familiarity with Jesus, the Author of faith, which made St Joseph the outstanding believer he was. For he shared his home with him who is the Light of the World, and in that heavenly radiance his faith became ever more luminous.

Paul VI proclaims in his Credo: "Jesus is the light; Mary is the lamp." From this latter source as well—the living lamp that lit up their Nazareth home—Joseph's faith drew constant illumination. As Newman points out, it was only to be expected that Joseph, through sheer proximity to his two all-holy treasures over so long a time, would himself become a giant in faith and holiness.

## REFERENCES FOR CHAPTER SIX
## JOSEPH, MAN OF FAITH

1...Votive Mass of St Joseph: Post-Communion prayer
2...Cardinal Peter d'Ailly: Tractatus de Sancto Josepho
3...John Paul II: Redemptoris Custos, 5
4...John Paul II: op. cit. 4
5...Pope St Leo the Great: PL 54, 191
6...Pius XII: Mystici Corporis

7...Christmas Mass: Preface Two
8...Leo XIII: Quamquam Pluries
9...St Thomas: Summa Contra Gentiles, IV, 27
10..St Thomas: Summa Theol: 1-25—6 (ad 4)
11..Pius XI: Address 19 March 1935
12..St Francis of Sales: Complete Works of St Francis of Sales, La Pleiade
13.. St Francis of Sales: Discourse 19, Complete Works of St Francis of Sales, VI

CHAPTER SEVEN

# JOSEPH, MAN OF GOD

On the occasion of his pilgrimage to Nazareth, Paul VI[1] described the Holy Family's home as "the school where one begins to understand the life of Jesus, that is, the school of the gospel." What can also be said of that sacred home-school is that there one begins to understand why and how the carpenter of Nazareth grew to be such a spiritual giant.

Many authorities have pointed out that, given the circumstances of Joseph's life and his mission in God's plan, he would as a matter of course have been blessed with a high degree of holiness. For he had been endowed with all the graces needed for his role as virginal father of the Redeemer and spouse of the Co-redemptrix. Over and above that, he steadily grew in holiness through his long-continued proximity and familiarity both with the Author of grace and his full-of-grace spouse. Small wonder, then, that, through spending all those years under the same roof with the Holy One of Israel and the Panhagia—Mary, the all-holy—and thus sharing their lives so intimately, the saint was mightily helped and inspired to scale the heights of holiness.

## Emmanuel's Physical Presence

Joseph's ongoing sanctification through being so close for so long to the God-Man throws a revealing sidelight on the mystery of the Incarnation. It does so by illustrating the fact that the Word Incarnate invariably distributed his favours to individuals through his humanity; that is, through the instrumentality of his bodily presence, his words, his deeds, his sufferings. St Thomas makes this point very clearly:[2]

67

**"It was by virtue of his divinity that Christ's human actions were salvific in our regard, producing grace within us either by merit or by a certain efficacy."**

This theme was taken up by John Paul II[3] with reference to St Joseph's sanctification, which, he explains, was enhanced and honed to a wonderful degree because of his physical closeness over the years to the sacred humanity. And this same "physical closeness" factor would later manifest itself during the Saviour's public ministry of sanctification and healing. An amazing early example is seen in the gospel episode we know as the Visitation. There it was the mere physical presence of Emmanuel, albeit still in his mother's womb, which caused that other unborn babe—the future John the Baptist—to "leap with joy" (cf. Lk 1: 41).

## The School of Nazareth

To return now to our opening point: St Joseph's dwelling-place in Nazareth functioned at the same time as a school of a very special kind—a school of the gospel, a school of holiness. Its Founder and Principal was the Word "who has the words of eternal life" (Jn 6: 68). And his first and all-time star pupils were (in this order) his mother and his legal father, themselves both destined to become leading models, tutors and guides for countless future Christian disciples in the centuries ahead.

As does every well-ordered school, the Nazareth one has a definite syllabus or curriculum; it was drawn up by the Founder, and he would subsequently formulate and preach it as the Christian gospel. Both doctrinal and moral teachings comprise the syllabus, which aims at instructing Christ's followers in revealed truth as well as promoting within them the imitation of the Master in thought, word and deed. In St Paul's summary phrase, the gospel-school trains disciples to "put on the mind of Christ" (cf. 1 Cor 2: 16).

It is in this context that Nazareth presents us with one of its many paradoxes: the Divine Apprentice who applied himself so diligently to obeying and learning his trade from Joseph was at the same time the spiritual Master and Exemplar from whom his guardian drew daily lessons in Christian wisdom and holiness. That is to say, the head of the Holy Family, during his long years of discipleship, was implicitly addressing the school's divine Founder in the prophetic words of their royal ancestor:

**"Direct my way, Lord, as thou wilt, teach me thy own paths. Ever let thy truth guide and teach me . . . Teach me goodness, discipline and knowledge, for I have believed thy commandments" (Ps 24: 4,5; 118: 66).**

### Joseph's All-Round Holiness

As we have been seeing, all tradition recognises that, among God's multitudinous holy ones, only the sinless Virgin Mary has surpassed Joseph in holiness of life. His unique brand of sanctity, says St Francis de Sales, combines the faith of the patriarchs, the light of confessors, and the strength of martyrs. In other words, the carpenter of Nazareth was second only to Mary in graduating with high distinction from the school conducted by their Son and Lord for all who believe in him. Moreover, Joseph's holiness was not only dazzling but comprehensive and all-inclusive; in a word, it exhibited the whole panoply of virtues and gifts distributed by the Holy Spirit.

Something of this all-round fullness is reflected in the Litany of St Joseph; it hails him as being, among other things, faithful, chaste, just, prudent, courageous, obedient, loyal, patient, industrious, pious, an exemplary parent, and a pillar of family life. It could be said, then, that the exhortation later to be addressed by St Paul to all Christians was amply fulfilled in advance by the "just man" of Nazareth: "Let the message of Christ, in all its richness, find a home in you" (Col 3: 16). Accordingly a good number of papal documents from Pius IX onwards have upheld St Joseph as a model of everything a follower of Christ is called to be. Benedict XV, for example, refers to his virtues as being "numerous and exalted," and this because "no virtue was lacking to ennoble the man who was to be the husband of Mary Immaculate and the foster-father of Jesus."[4]

## The Anatomy of Holiness

In order to assess the depth and richness of Joseph's interior life, we first need to ask ourselves what holiness basically means. One can appropriately speak of its having an anatomy, since holiness is, in actual fact, a form of life—life of a very precious kind, being nothing less than God's own life in which we are privileged to share. The technical name for this life is grace, sanctifying grace, and this it is that the Son of God had in mind when he declared: "I have come that they may have life, and have it more abundantly" (Jn 10: 10).

Being a participation in Christ's own life, grace produces Christlikeness, alias holiness, within its recipients, ennobling and consecrating them as temples of worship, prayer and devotion. From this it follows that the degree of anyone's holiness is determined by the amount of grace they possess. What also follows is that Mary, being full of grace besides being God's mother, is his top-ranking masterpiece of holiness.

As for Mary's spouse, he was the next-ranking masterpiece of holiness formed at Nazareth with such loving care by the Saviour. Through the divine life with which Joseph was so superabundantly endowed, every fibre of his being, his every thought, word and action, each single duty, trial and cross that came his way—in sum, every tiny detail of his life—was sanctified through being caught up into the supernatural sphere of grace and merit.

## In the Service of Grace

As was to be the case with all baptised Christians, Christ's earthly father received, along with sanctifying grace, the complete spiritual apparatus, so to call it, that equips us for prayer and the other operations and activities proper to our supernatural status.

This spiritual apparatus or equipment is manifold, comprising first and foremost the three theological virtues of faith, hope and charity. Hereby Joseph was enabled respectively to see and appreciate the living reality of God and his invisible kingdom; to desire and aspire towards God and his kingdom with a burning longing and complete confidence in the divine goodness; and, most important of all, to love God with the love of his whole heart, mind, soul and strength, and his neighbour as himself.

Again as is the case with all baptised Christians, further virtues — the so-called moral ones: namely, prudence, justice, fortitude and temperance — were infused by God the Sanctifier into Joseph's soul, each of them designed to promote and facilitate in its distinctive way the operations of grace.

### Gifts of the Holy Spirit

Likewise forming part of the supernatural apparatus, and designed to promote and facilitate in souls the operations of grace, is the Holy Spirit's sevenfold gift — wisdom, understanding, counsel, knowledge, fortitude, piety and fear of the Lord. Each after its own particular fashion, the gifts enhance the effectiveness of the virtues we receive along with grace, especially in difficult and trying situations.

These gifts of the Spirit, which St Joseph received in such full neasure, made him a pliant and generous instrument in the Lord's service. Wisdom enabled him to discern with great clarity God's presence and designs in all things and at all times. Through the gift of understanding he was enlightened to penetrate the inner meaning of sacred scripture, particularly those texts relating to the life and destiny of the Messiah entrusted to his care. And when the saint found himself beset by problems and crises arising from his demanding duties and concerns, the Holy Spirit's gift of counsel proved invaluable. As for fortitude, it supported the Redeemer's guardian amid the many dangers, difficulties and obstacles he had to face.

A happy characteristic of these supernatural gifts is that, provided we remain faithful to God, they increase as we go through life. So, too, for that matter, do all the various endowments forming part of the spiritual apparatus. The reason is that they are closely associated with and subsidiary to divine grace; and grace, being a form of created life — indeed, the highest possible — is a dynamic reality that seeks of itself to grow. St Peter was aware of this. "Grow up in grace," he exhorts us (2 Pet. 3: 18). And St John the Baptist meant much the same thing when he said of the Author of Grace: "He must increase, and I must decrease" (Jn 3: 30).

## Just and Obedient

That St Joseph was a "just man" we know from Scripture. The Church widens the compliment by referring to him as "the just and obedient man" to whom the Father entrusted his Incarnate Son.[5]

What we learn from this is that St Joseph was totally submissive to the divine will. This is evident from the prompt and unquestioning way he carried out God's instructions conveyed to him on several occasions through mystical agencies. His meat and his drink, he could say with the Saviour, was at all times to do the will of the heavenly Father (cf. Jn 4: 34). And like his beloved spouse, the Lord's handmaid, Joseph conformed his entire life, down to its smallest details, "according to God's word" (cf. Lk 1: 38).

Pope St Gregory the Great said of obedience that it is not just a virtue but the mother of all virtues. This explains why the ever-obedient Joseph attained the heights of holiness in its every department. Obedience to God was the solid bedrock upon which his entire lifework rested. Or to put it another way, the divine will was the lodestar of his life. He was "just," says St Francis of Sales, essentially because he was united with the will of God.

In the first place, this meant keeping God's commandments with scrupulous care and faithfully observing the rules, rites and ordinances of Israel. It further meant complete fidelity to the promptings and warnings of conscience, that inner, divine voice which Newman describes as "the messenger from him who in nature and in grace speaks to us behind a veil."

Incidentally, it was largely from St Joseph's inspiring example that one of his closest clients — St Jane Frances de Chantal — made it a rule of life that God's will must at all costs be done, "with no ifs, no buts, and no exceptions." What she further learned from St Joseph is that our wayward, wilful selves need to be totally submitted to the divine will if we are to make progress in the school of holiness. What God wills, St Paul declares, is our sanctification (cf.I Thess 4: 3). But the reverse of this formula is equally true: our sanctification lies in obeying God's will.

## Man of Prayer

Amid the silence that shrouds Joseph in the gospels, says John Paul II,[6] one can discern in him "an aura of contemplation" from the fact, the awe-inspiring fact, that, actually dwelling with him under his roof and sharing his daily toil and bread alike, was "the mystery hidden from ages past" (Col 1: 26). Consequently their Nazareth home was virtually heaven on earth for the Holy Family. Newman[7] had this in mind when he likened prayer to "the language of heaven and an exercise of our citizenship there."

In view of all this, few would disagree with St Bernardine of Siena that the Saviour's guardian is second only to the Virgin Mother as a contemplative. For, sharing his home and the intimacies of domestic life, was the God-Man in person, the Eternal Word communing unbrokenly with his Heavenly Father. Also forming part of Joseph's life was his beloved spouse, Emmanuel's all-holy mother, whose great hymn of praise, the Magnificat, testifies to her being Israel's Mystical Rose and House of Gold.

It was only to be expected, then, that in such a spiritual ambience Joseph's prayer-life progressively developed beyond all telling. His union with God was close and continuous. And, as he went about his humdrum routines, he embodied the maxim later coined by St Francis of Sales for the benefit of all those enrolled in the Lord's school of holiness: "Give him your heart a thousand times a day."

## St Joseph's Prayer

Like everyone else's, St Joseph's prayer would necessarily have fallen into the four main kinds that express mankind's basic religious duties and needs; we know them as adoration, contrition, intercession and thanksgiving. Now nowhere does this foursome find such classic expression as in that great treasury of prayer—the Old Testament psalms. To a devout Israelite like St Joseph they would have provided a wealth of texts to meet and match life's changing patterns and moods.

The dominant mode of prayer for St Joseph was unquestionably adoration; after all, he shared his home and much of his life with the God of heaven and earth clothed in flesh as human as his own. One particular psalm-verse could well have found a constant echo in Joseph's heart: "At all times I will bless the Lord; his praise shall be on my lips continually" (Ps 3: 2).

As does every prayer, adoration, Augustine observes, flows from faith as from a fountain. Now because the faith the Nazareth carpenter had in the Incarnation was flame-like in its intensity, it imparted a unique purity and power to his adoration of the Word-made-flesh. Indeed, nobody except Mary has more ardently than he worshipped the God-Man "in spirit and in truth" (Jn 4: 24).

Though a minority view holds that one of St Joseph's privileges was his lifelong preservation from all personal sins, it seems more likely that the prayer of contrition, howsoever minor his offences may have been, did in fact find a place in Joseph's prayer-life. Here again a whole array of psalm-prayers would have served his purpose, particularly King David's great act of contrition and plea for forgiveness as found in psalm 50. Its opening verse goes to the very heart of the matter: "Have mercy on me, O God, as thou art ever rich in mercy; in the abundance of thy compassion blot out the record of my misdeeds" (Ps 50: 3).

We can be sure that the third kind of prayer—intercession or petition—played a major part in St Joseph's spiritual life, especially in times of trial and crisis. Two prominent instances were the flight into Egypt and the loss in the temple. Faced with these crises, the Lord's earthly guardian could appropriately have made the psalmist's plea his own: "O God, our Saviour, help us; deliver us, Lord, for the glory of thy name" (Ps 78:9).

As regards the prayer of thanksgiving, the saint would have made it frequently and fervently. In all likelihood he used for this purpose Mary's great prayer of gratitude—the Magnificat. Also he would have recalled many apposite psalm-verses expressive of our thankfulness to God for his multiple benefits. One particular text was a favourite with the people of Israel: "Bless the Lord, my soul, remembering all he has done for thee . . . how he heals all thy mortal ills . . . how he crowns thee with the blessings of his mercy . . . how he contents all thy desire for good" (Ps 102: 2-5).

## Man of Peace

"Peace is the seed-ground of holiness" (St James, 3:18). From this text we may infer that St Joseph's peace of mind must have been of the highest order for it to produce in him such a harvest of holiness. Already he had been singularly blessed with this heavenly gift when the Bethlehem angels heralded the arrival on earth of the Prince of Peace. And, during the years ahead, that Prince continued to enrich his guardian with this heavenly treasure, which he would later bequeath to his disciples as a precious legacy (cf. Jn 14: 27).

How integral peace is to the Christian scheme of things is evident from the frequency with which the theme occurs throughout the New Testament and in the Church's liturgy, notably the Mass. Peace is no less integral to Christian spirituality, as is well exemplified in the interior life of the saints.

Peace was well defined by St Augustine[8] as "the tranquillity of order in the human spirit." Which order, as we can all verify through personal experience, applies at three levels: in our relations with the God of conscience; within our own body-soul selves; and in our relations with our fellow-humans. Let us now apply these three categories to St Joseph.

His relations with the God of conscience were of the purest and holiest. Being a "just man," he carefully avoided sin and its occasions. Moreover, his close family life with the sinless Word Incarnate and the immaculate virgin daily reinforced his resolve to exclude any thought, word or deed that would offend the all-holy Lord of the commandments and so stain his conscience.

From peace with the God of conscience, and from it alone, flows peace within our inmost selves, peace of mind and imagination, peace of body. This is the peace that reigned in St Joseph at all times, no matter what life cared to throw at him by way of outer disturbances, mishaps, disappointments, sufferings or whatever else.

Thirdly, St Joseph's relations with others. Here the two other members of his family come directly into focus. The deep, undisturbed peace that united Joseph in his Nazareth home with the Prince of Peace and its queen inspired the Church's liturgical prayer: "Father, we want to live as Jesus, Mary and Joseph in peace with you and one another."[9]

## The Joy of the Lord

Joy has been called "the keynote of the Christian message." This is already evident from Our Lord's words to his apostles: "All this I have told you so that my joy may be yours" (Jn 15: 11). And in the lives of the saints we see how characteristically the joy of the Lord manifested itself. Very significantly, one of the Church's criteria for canonisation is precisely that candidates should have evidenced consistent joyousness during their lives.

In this light, then, we may safely assume that the greatest of the saints after Mary was throughout his life a model of divine joy. And we may further assume that his joy constantly increased during those many years he spent in close daily contact with joy's Source and Giver, and with her whom we hail as Cause of our Joy.

From St Joseph's example the Lord's followers can learn that joy, besides being a privilege, is something we must assiduously work at and cultivate. St Paul lays emphasis on this. "Rejoice in the Lord always," he writes, "and again I say rejoice" (Phil 4: 4). The point about the word "always" in this context is that it refers not just to all times but to all of life's circumstances.

Now life's circumstances, as no one knew better from hard experience than the head of the Holy Family, are apt to be changeful and can be most difficult and trying. In the poet's words, "life will mingle thee rue and roses." Unwanted evils like pain, suffering and sorrow can without the least warning or compunction spread the darkest clouds across life's landscape.

Though many such clouds came to overshadow Joseph's life, his inner joy remained undisturbed. For he was united inseparably with the God of joy. Thus, paradoxically, joy co-existed in him undisturbed alongside whatever pain of mind or body came his way. Herein he exemplified Newman's[10] maxim: "Gloom is no Christian temper. We must live in sunshine even when we sorrow." Or as the Cure d'Ars used to say: "For a soul that loves God, it is forever springtime."

Another golden value of Christian joy to be learned from St Joseph is that it can transcend and sanctify pain and sorrow, precisely through being offered to God in reparation for our own sins or coredemptively for the sins of others. As St Paul later formulated this key truth, we can and do rejoice in our sufferings, for thereby we fill up what is lacking in the sufferings of Christ for his body, the Church (cf. I Col 1: 24).

### REFERENCES FOR CHAPTER SEVEN
### JOSEPH, MAN OF GOD

1...Paul VI: Discourse at Nazareth, January 5, 1964
2...St Thomas: Summa Theol, 3-8-1 (ad I)
3...John Paul II: Redemptoris Custos, 27
4...Benedict XV: Bonum Sane
5 ..Votive Mass of St Joseph: Post-Communion prayer
6...John Paul II: op. cit. 25
7...Cardinal John Henry Newman: Pastoral and Parochial Sermons, IV, 228-229
8...St Augustine: City of God, XIII, 19
9...Feast of the Holy Family: Post-Communion
10..Cardinal John Henry Newman: op. cit. V, 271

# St. Joseph, Patron of the Triumph

CHAPTER EIGHT

# JOSEPH'S SORROWS AND DEATH

**B**eing descended like ourselves from mankind's first parents, St Joseph contracted from them the guilt of original sin. But as to when he was purified from this hereditary guilt nothing is known for certain. Did it take place, as happened with John the Baptist, when Joseph was still in his mother's womb? Among the many authorities who think it did are two canonised doctors of the Church, Francis of Sales and Alphonsus Liguori.

Again like everyone else, Joseph contracted from Adam and Eve their sin's penal consequences, the most calamitous of which were, of course, the loss of divine grace and the resultant shipwreck of our eternal destiny. But both these dire penalties were cancelled out for St Joseph when he was purified from our ancestral guilt.

What St Joseph further had in common with his fellow-humans is that he was subject to the rest of original sin's penal consequences; these came into effect when the Creator withdrew certain privileges he had generously conferred on our protoparents and their entire progeny. Because these privileges greatly enhanced man's natural capacities, they went by the name of preternatural. Two of them—each designed to provide us with an invaluable immunity—specifically concern us here. The first immunity was from suffering and sorrow during our lifetime, the second from death at its end.

As Christian piety has from earliest days assumed that St Joseph was privileged to die in the presence of the Word Incarnate and Mary, he is traditionally associated with the grace of a happy death and is invoked as its special patron. We shall presently be looking at the saint's death and the devotion that has built up around it. So it will be helpful if beforehand we see something of death's place and meaning in God's overall plan.

The same applies to sorrow and suffering, both of which featured to no small extent in Joseph's divine mission. Therefore a preliminary look at these sombre realities will help us to appreciate more keenly how they fitted into Joseph's role as head of the Holy Family.

## The Prince of Death

As the saint would have known from the Book of Wisdom, death's instigator and ruler is the devil, who was motivated thereto by envy towards God's human creation (cf. Wis 2: 23-24). Certainly the Creator had not intended that we humans should die, mortal though our bodies are of themselves. John Paul II says apropos of this:

**"God could not have created death because, as Scripture says, he cannot delight in the destruction of the living (cf. Wis 1: 3). God's original plan was impeded by sin, since he created man for incorruption and made him the image of his own eternity."[1]**

Because the devil's subtle temptation was largely to blame for humanity's primordial fall, the letter to the Hebrews aptly styles him "the prince of death." But it goes on to assure us that the Son of God deposed him through his own death, thereby delivering us from all fear of this evil (Heb 2: 14-15). As St Joseph was to see for himself at painfully close range, the prince of death, deploying the infamous King Herod as his instrument, aimed to secure another signal victory by plotting the premature death of the infant Lord of Life. But, through the agency of his faithful guardian, the new-born Redeemer was delivered from the hands of the murderous tyrant.

However, the Redeemer was not destined in later years to be delivered from that cruellest of all deaths—crucifixion. Incidentally, both he and Joseph would have been familiar with this form of capital punishment; in their day it was quite common to see convicted men dying upon crosses. Indeed, Christ would probably have been about 10 years old when no less than 2,000 prisoners were crucified in the vicinity of his hometown under orders from the Roman general Varus. Their crime had been an attempted raid on an armoury in Sepphoris, which lay just beyond the crest of the hill overlooking Nazareth.

## The Dominion of Death

So it is as a penal consequence of Adam and Eve's sin that the human race is now "subject to the dominion of death."[2] Man, the composite of spirit and matter, and now stripped of his preternatural immunity from death, is as God made him—an immortal spirit united with a mortal body. Which accounts for the rock-bottom certainty that every individual without exception must and will die. (cf. Heb 9: 27). Shakespeare found words for this stark hometruth:[3]

**"Golden lads and girls all must,
As chimney-sweepers, come to dust."**

By a strange paradox, death's certainty is matched by an equal uncertainty regarding its when and its how. Hence Our Lord's exhortation that we be at all times prepared to exit from this world in his friendship (cf.Mt 25: 13).

As for Our Lord's own exit from this world, it established for us an entrance into God's kingdom of everlasting life and love. For he died as our Redeemer, having been enabled to fulfil that mission, thanks in great part to the faithful custodian who, from his infancy onwards, had shielded, nourished, guided and fathered him.

Furthermore, the Saviour's redeeming death has wrought a transformation in how we now regard our own eventual demise from this world. Death is no longer the horror, the terror, the taboo subject, "the last enemy" of which St Paul speaks (I Cor 15: 26). Christ has overthrown it so completely and triumphantly that we can all make our own the Pauline claim: "Life means Christ, and death is a prize to be won" (Phil 1: 21). And, too, we can join with St Francis of Assisi in hailing death as "our little sister who opens for us the gate of life."

## All Our Woes

The dominion of death ushered in by Original Sin extends to all the sufferings and sorrows that are so liable to afflict us, often enough without a moment's notice, as we journey through life. Thus in his aptly-titled *Paradise Lost,* John Milton speaks of:[4]

**"Man's first disobedience and the fruit
Of that forbidden tree, whose mortal taste
Brought death to the world, and all our woes,
With loss of Eden."**

As St Joseph learned for himself in life's hard school, human woes come in two forms — spiritual and bodily; that is, suffering of the body and sorrow in the mind. Bodily sufferings can be trivial or tremendous, passing or permanent, merely inconveniencing or totally incapacitating. They can range from headaches and cancer to hernias and the hideous injuries apt to arise from road accidents. Spiritual sufferings, on the other hand, wound us inwardly, and can do so in ways and to degrees quite as wide-ranging as the bodily variety. Here we think of things like worry, loneliness, fear, disappointments, bereavements. Interior sufferings like these transform the garden of the soul into a little Gethsamene, while the bodily kind look to Calvary as their crowning summit.

Scripture says of the Lord who so lovingly endured everything that Gethsamene and Calvary could inflict on him: "Son of God though he was, he learned obedience in the school of suffering" (Heb 5: 8). Obedience basically means our loving acceptance of God's will. This is the paramount lesson we pupils in life's school of suffering are to master at all costs.

A further key lesson in the syllabus is that every suffering, whatever its shape or size, really forms part of the penalty that the sins of the world, our own included, justly deserve for our having offended against the Almighty Creator. Indeed, that crucified pair who flanked our Saviour on Good Friday can be said to represent all of us, since everyone without exception hangs on a cross carpentered by life's circumstances. But we must at all costs identify

Joseph's Sorrows and Death

with the Good Thief by saying to the Crucified Lord: "We suffer these things justly on account of our sins" (Lk 23: 41).

Yet another key lesson is that we can offer our Redeemer every sorrow and suffering that comes our way as a coredemptive contribution to the salvation of souls. This is what St Paul meant when he said that he filled up in his own body what was still lacking in the sufferings of Christ—and this for the good of Christ's mystical body, the Church (cf. Col 1: 24).

**Heartaches and Shocks**

Through being so close to the pair destined to become respectively the Man and the Mother of Sorrows, Joseph was drawn deep into their redemptive mission while he toiled over the years in their service. And, precisely through his closeness and cooperation, he found himself called to suffer in numerous ways "the heartache and the thousand natural shocks that flesh is heir to."[5]

Basing itself on the gospel narratives, Christian piety has gathered into a litany the seven major sorrows in the early stages of St Joseph's guardian-role. The first was a deep and wounding heartache, since it concerned his own beloved spouse's mysterious pregnancy. Joseph was tortured by perplexity and pain of mind as to how he should proceed in the circumstances until, dramatically and mercifully, the Lord's angel resolved his spiritual crisis.

The ensuing Bethlehem episode came initially as a most trying experience for the young spouses. Besides the heavy inconvenience involved in getting there from Nazareth, particularly for an expectant mother, they faced a last-minute accommodation problem rendered all the more acute by the imminence of Mary's confinement. To Joseph's mortification he finally had to settle for the rough shelter of a cattle-byre as the birthplace of the Messiah.

The circumcision of Jesus likewise occasioned a sorrow for his virginal father. Knowing that, according to the Scriptures, the Infant Messiah would one day suffer at the hands of sinful men, Joseph felt a pang of compassion and presentiment on seeing the precious blood shed for the first time. And he felt a similar pang when, some weeks later, at the presentation in the temple, Simeon prophesied not only that the Child would encounter bitter opposition but that his mother's heart would be pierced by a sword of sorrow.

King Herod's threat on the new-born Saviour's life brought yet another heavy sorrow into Joseph's life. He led his two precious charges to safety—but at the same time into enforced exile—in Egypt. When they finally returned, they took up their abode in Nazareth, having been warned in the meantime of a further potential threat on the Child's life by Herod's son now reigning in Judea.

The final recorded sorrow Joseph experienced during the early years of the hidden life was the loss of the Child Jesus in the temple. We cannot imagine what grief and anxiety filled the hearts of his sorrowing parents during their three-day search, the more so as they remembered how his life had been threatened here in Judea during the Massacre of the Innocents. Nor can we imagine what relief and joy flooded their souls when they finally found their missing Son.

## The Circumstances of Joseph's Death

Though the actual circumstances of the saint's death are unknown, we may confidently surmise that it took place in his Nazareth home and was attended by Jesus and Mary. What is equally likely is that Joseph died before Our Lord's public ministry began. For, had her spouse still been alive, Mary would not have been free to accompany her Messiah-Son on his missionary journeys. In that case her presence and role as Co-redemptrix at the side of the Redeemer would have been obscured, especially on Good Friday.

Moreover, Christ's listeners would have been confused to hear him speak about his heavenly Father (as he so often did) if his putative father had still been alive. But the really clinching argument is that, shortly before leaving this world, the Crucified Saviour confided his mother to the care of John the Evangelist, clearly indicating thereby that she was a widow (cf. Jn 19: 26-27).

What convinced St Bernardine of Siena that Joseph died prior to Christ's public life is that God, the all-merciful Father, called him to himself betimes so as to spare him the grief that would have overwhelmed him on account of the bitter passion of the man he loved as his Son and worshipped as his God.

No facts at all are available regarding what may have caused Joseph's death. St Francis of Sales was convinced that he actually died of the love of God. The text in question reads:[6]

**"A saint who had loved so much during his life could not die save of love. And, having completed the office for which he was destined, it only remained for him to say to the Eternal Father, 'I have completed the task you gave me to do'; and to the Son, 'O my Child, as your heavenly Father placed your body in my hands the day you came into this world, so now, on this day of my departure from this world, I place my soul in your hands.' Such, I conceive, was the death of this great patriarch."**

St Francis' reasoning is supported by the testimony of several mystics besides being fully endorsed by Alphonsus Liguori, his fellow-saint and fellow-doctor of the Church.[7]

Interestingly enough, St Francis of Sales went on to advance the same view with regard to Mary's death; it was "a transport of love," he claimed, that brought it about. In other words, "Mary died in love, from love, and through love for her Son Jesus."[8]

## Joseph's Deathbed

In his meditation on Joseph's death, Cardinal Newman spoke of the deep understanding and sympathy that united the dying man with his two dear ones, at whom he now gazed "with an undivided, unreserved, supreme devotion, for he was in the arms of God and the mother of God."[9]

We can imagine those closing moments of Joseph's life. His crucial role as Emmanuel's personal guardian was fast nearing its consummation. Soon he would hear those welcoming words from the Lord of life and death: "Well done, thou good and faithful servant" (Mt 25: 21).

Thus it was Joseph's crowning privilege to be personally assisted in his last agony by that same Divine Lord—the Great High Priest himself—who would be pronouncing the above welcome. The paradoxical reversal of roles about to take place between father and Son is well expressed in the devotional hymn to St Joseph:

> **"O blest reward, when in his arms,**
> **You sighed your dying breath.**
> **You cradled Jesus at his birth,**
> **He cradled you at death."**

This was the Lord who would later weep over the death of his friend Lazarus. Therefore with even more reason he would have done the same over this just man who had with a father's love protected and nurtured him in those distant days of infancy and boyhood; this just man whose whole life and mission had been to minister to him as the Saviour and so promote the mysteries of redemption; this just man who had so devotedly loved and served his mother Mary as her dedicated spouse; this just man whose holiness was second only to that of the all-holy virgin herself; this just man who would one day be honoured as patron of the Universal Church; this just man to whom the psalmist's words could now so aptly be applied: "Precious in the eyes of the Lord is the death of those who love him" (Ps 115: 6).

### Patron of a Happy Death

A time-honoured popular hymn by an anonymous author proclaims:

> **"To all who would holily live,**
> **To all who would happily die,**
> **St Joseph is ready to give**
> **Sure guidance and help from on high."**

St Joseph is deservedly patron of a happy death because his own was the paradigm, the shining exemplar, of what dying holily and peacefully in the Lord is meant to be. Accordingly we must ask him, frequently and fervently, to obtain for us the supreme grace of final perseverance and thus of dying in God's friendship and peace. Meanwhile the official patron of a happy death offers us much "sure guidance and help" on this subject. First of all, he encourages us to look forward to death as "a prize to be won" (Phil 1: 21) now that the God-Man's sacrifice on our behalf has "transformed the curse of death into a blessing."[10]

Secondly, St Joseph exemplified the Ignatian adage that we believers are called to glorify God even more through our death than through our life. For is not our death a participation in the Lord's, being the last opportunity we shall have for gaining merit? Therefore we must make of it a masterpiece, as did St Joseph. What this demands in the first place is that we duly prepare to exit from this world by living at all times in a state of grace. For we know neither the day nor the hour when that most ruthless and uncompromising of thieves will come to rob us of our bodily life (cf. Mt 25: 13).

A further lesson we can learn from the patron of a happy death is that by a strange paradox our deathday will be, in Lacordaire's words, "the most beautiful day of our lives." For in effect it will be our birthday into the heavenly world God has prepared for those who love him. We find this same truth expressed by King Solomon in the form of a proverb: "Man's true birthday is the day of his death" (Ecclesiastes 7: 2). And the early Christians crystallized the identical belief into one of their favourite epitaphs: "dies natalis"—the joyously triumphant happy-birthday greeting we find inscribed a thousandfold in the Roman catacombs.

What St Joseph's death also guarantees is that ours, too, will be attended and sanctified not only by Mary but by him who is the Resurrection and the Life (cf. Jn 11: 25). And, what is more, at the end of time the Risen Saviour "will form this humbled body of ours anew, moulding it into the image of his glorified body" (Phil 3: 21). Death's sting and the grave's victory will have been vanquished forever.

## Deathbed Shadows

St Bernadette used to say that because our death has been transfigured by Christ, it will be the greatest personal act we can offer God in this world. Nevertheless it will never altogether lose the penal aspect it took on as a consequence of original sin. So for nobody, St Joseph included, could the death-experience ever prove to be unalloyed sweetness and light. Certain shadows will inevitably fall over any and every deathbed scene, howsoever abundantly God's peace and love may preside there.

First of these shadows is our instinctive fear of death. Not even he who died in the presence of Emmanuel and immaculate Mary was fully exempt from it. For he was a human being, and his spirit accordingly experienced a natural repugnance at the very thought of separation from its faithful partner down the years—the body.

So it arises that the inescapable prospect of death can and often does pose a challenge to our peace of soul and trust in God. St Francis of Sales was sensitively aware of this problem and sought to allay it in the minds of his spiritual children. His words of wisdom and counsel were inspired by his filial devotion to the Saviour's guardian:[11]

**"Often fill your mind with thoughts of the great gentleness and mercy with which God our Saviour welcomes those souls at death who have spent their lives in trusting him and have striven to love him and serve him. Do your utmost to arouse in yourself a love of heaven and the life of the blessed in order to weaken your dread of parting from this mortal and fleeting life."**

Another shadow of an even more sinister kind hanging over every deathbed is cast by the fallen angels, envious of us as they are till our very last breath. St Alphonsus Liguori, in his reflection on the title "terror of demons" conferred on Joseph by the Church, offers us these words of comfort:

"St Joseph is most powerful against the demons who fight against us at the end of our lives. Jesus has granted to him the special privilege of safeguarding the dying against the snares of Lucifer, just as he also saved Jesus from the schemes of Herod. St Joseph's privilege is to obtain for his faithful servants a holy and peaceful death, and those who invoke him in their final hour will be comforted by, and enjoy the assistance of, Jesus and Mary."[12]

The third shadow hovering over our deathbed arises from our lack of patience while we await death's arrival. Not that there is anything wrong in saying with St Paul: "I long to be dissolved and to be with Christ" (Phil 1: 23). But we fall short of the Christian ideal if we grow impatient with Little Sister Death's delay, as can happen with invalids and sufferers longing to be relieved of their cross. Let us never forget that it is for the Lord of life and death, and for him alone, to decide how and when we leave this world. "Be patient," St James urges, "until the coming of the Lord...which is at hand" (James 5: 7-8).

A striking example of this attitude was St Bernadette of Lourdes; amid her sufferings she frequently asked her beloved St Joseph for the grace not only of a happy death but of patience in awaiting its advent. Teresa of Avila did likewise. "I want to see God," she wrote, "and in order to see him I must die." However, the timing of that happy event, this loving daughter of St Joseph fully accepted, is exclusively for God to decide.

Cardinal Newman drew that same lesson from his meditation on the death of St Joseph. While looking forward to our own death as the gateway to eternal life, we must resign ourselves totally to God's will as to when and how it comes. But there is consolation as well as resignation about the prospect: "Not a day passes but I am nearer the goal. I am ever narrowing the interval between time and eternity."[13]

## REFERENCES FOR CHAPTER EIGHT
## JOSEPH'S SUFFERINGS AND DEATH

1...John Paul II: General Audience Address (reported in L'Osservatore Romano, June 9, 1999)
2...Council of Trent: Decree on Original Sin, Denz. 1511-1551
3...William Shakespeare: Cymbeline, iv, 2
4...John Milton: Paradise Lost, Bk 1
5...William Shakespeare: Hamlet, III, 1
6...St Francis of Sales: Treatise on the Love of God, Bk 7, ch 13
7...St Alphonsus Liguori: Meditation on the Death of St Joseph
8...St Francis of Sales: ibid.
9...Cardinal John Henry Newman: Meditations and Devotions
10..Catechism of the Catholic Church: # 1009
11..St Francis of Sales: ibid.
12..St Alphonsus Liguori: Exhortation for Increase of Devotion to St Joseph
13..Cardinal John Henry Newman: ibid

# CHAPTER NINE

# DEVOTION TO JOSEPH

**M**ention has been made in earlier pages of certain special privileges enjoyed by St Joseph; they served either to prepare or
reward him for his vital part in the mysteries of redemption. Many
authors, including several doctors of the Church and canonised
saints, have speculated about these privileges, which began with
the purification of the Redeemer's custodian from original sin while
still in his mother's womb—as was likewise to be the case with the
Redeemer's precursor.

Joseph's next privilege was his preservation from personal
sin and immunity from concupiscence—a privilege specifically
designed for someone called to spend long years of close family
intimacy with the Holy One of Israel and his sinless mother. Here
the question arises: did this privilege apply from the very first
moment St Joseph enjoyed the use of reason? Or did it become
operative only when he was confirmed in grace on marrying the
Co-redemptrix of all graces? Opinions are divided on this point.

Joseph's crowning privilege was, of course, his bodily resurrection and assumption into heavenly glory. Few would disagree
that it is reasonable to include the Saviour's earthly father among
"those holy men gone to their rest" who rose from their graves at
Christ's resurrection and were seen by many in Jerusalem (cf. Mt
27: 52). More than that, we are assured by St Thomas, among others, that Joseph's glorified humanity was subsequently taken up
into heaven on Ascension Thursday along with those others who
had risen with Christ on Easter Sunday.

No one has championed Joseph's privileges more enthusia-
stically than St Francis of Sales. Regarding his assumption he wrote:[1]

**"We must never doubt that the glorious St. Joseph
wields great influence in heaven with him who favoured
him to the point of raising him body and soul. This**

**seems all the more probable imasmuch as we possess no relic of him here below on earth . . . Doubtless on descending into Limbo Our Lord was hailed thus by St Joseph: 'My Lord, recall, if you please, that when you came on earth from heaven I received you into my house and my family. Receive me into yours now that you are going there. I carried you in my arms; so now take me in yours. And as I undertook to feed and guide you in the course of your mortal life, take care of me and lead me to life immortal.'"**

### Patron of the Church

When in 1870 Pius IX declared St Joseph patron and guardian of the universal Church, he was not newly appointing him to this position but was simply promulgating a privileged function that the saint had exercised as of right from the beginning. For Leo XIII[2] had already made clear that Joseph is the Church's patron in virtue of his being the husband of Mary, the father of Jesus, and head of the holy family. What this amounts to saying is that the Church is mystically the extension of the Lord's Nazareth family across space and time. As the pontiff went on to explain:

**"The divine household which Joseph governed with paternal authority contained the beginnings of the new Church . . . The Virgin most holy is the mother of all Christians . . . And Jesus is as it were the first-born of all Christians, who are his brothers by adoption and redemption. Hence we conclude that the blessed patriarch must regard the multitude of Christians who constitute the Church as being confided to his care in a certain special manner . . . The Church is St Joseph's family beyond number, scattered throughout all lands, over which he rules with a sort of paternal authority."**

No less deeply aware of St Joseph's close patronal links with the universal Church was John XXIII. In fact, this prompted him to declare him heavenly protector of the Second Vatican Council, realising as he already did that the Church's overall well-being and modernisation would have top priority on its agenda.

Interestingly enough, it was in one of the Council's initial sessions that John XXIII had occasion to give striking proof of the high esteem in which he held St Joseph. For it so happened that a certain Yugoslav bishop felt moved to stand up and express his regret to the assembled prelates that devotion to St Joseph had sadly declined in the present-day Church. This statement evoked a chorus of derisive laughter from the assembly: after all, was it for trivial matters such as this that they had been summoned to Rome from the ends of the earth?

We can imagine how chastised many of those worthies must have felt when, the very next day (November 13, 1962), Cardinal Cicognani, speaking on the Holy Father's behalf, solemnly announced that he had decided to pay St Joseph the signal honour of including him, with immediate effect, in the canon of the Roman Mass, his name to be placed immediately after the Virgin Mary's and ahead of John the Baptist, the apostles and martyrs.

## Keeping the Faith

Undoubtedly one of St Joseph's prime concerns as patron of the Church is that it faithfully preserves and safeguards the precious truths of revelation—the so-called deposit of faith. Let us recall that the carpenter of Nazareth had been further privileged, along with Mary, to be the first depositary of two key New Testament truths: her virginal conception, and her Child's identity as the Incarnate Son of God and Redeemer-to-be of fallen mankind.

The truly prodigious quality of Joseph's faith is evidenced in the unquestioning way he accepted from God a series of revelations and communications that were stunning in themselves and steeped in the profoundest mystery. Like Mary, he treasured these precious truths and pondered them continuously in his heart (cf. Lk 2: 19). And here that special gift of the Holy Spirit we know as understanding would have enabled him to penetrate ever more deeply into these and all revealed doctrines.

How appropriate, then, it is that Joseph is patron of "the household of faith," as St Paul designates the Church (Gal 6: 10). For its whole secret is that it was founded and commissioned by God to communicate to mankind the precious truths of faith. We see this reflected in the question put to baptisands: "What do you ask of the Church of God?" To which their set reply is: "Faith."

So we should frequently petition the Church's universal patron that it remain ever faithful to its sacred commission and commitment, and that its teaching authority (the so-called magisterium) be heeded and honoured by all. Furthermore, St Joseph's intercession is particularly needed nowadays on behalf of those who obstinately oppose and obstruct the magisterium. This they do by doubting, distorting or denying certain dogmatic and moral truths. What is still more serious and sinful, they abuse their often influential positions by spreading their errors to others.

A very grave responsibility in this matter obviously falls to the Church's hierarchical leaders. Their surest way of demonstrating obedience to the God of revelation is by ensuring that all under their jurisdiction — not least those who teach the sacred sciences — remain loyal to the Church's magisterial authority. For nothing is more urgently important than that the authentic faith as articulated in the Catholic Catechism be faithfully transmitted at every level — school, seminary and university.

Indeed, St Ambrose[3] sees in Joseph the type of the Church's hierarchical leaders called to lead the faithful in truth and holiness. Correspondingly the sovereign pontiff and all bishops in union with him should recognise in the Church's patron a model and inspiration for their own exercise of authority over the precious souls entrusted to their care. Just how precious they truly are was well expressed by another great leader in the Church's early days — St John Chrysostom, likewise a staunch client of its universal patron. "One soul," he stated, not least for the benefit of his fellow-hierarchs, "is diocese enough for a bishop."

## Spreading the Faith

But it is not the hierarchy alone who should be concerned with the preservation and spread of the Catholic faith. In an apostolic letter issued some ten years after Vatican II, Pope Paul VI[4] directed an urgent appeal to every single member of the Church, asking them to reflect earnestly on their God-given mission to propagate the treasures of faith with which we have been enriched by the Son of Mary and Joseph. "Evangelization," he reminded us, "is the grace and vocation proper to the Church, her deepest identity. She exists in order to evangelize."

This papal call has since been repeatedly echoed by John Paul II. And, as did Paul VI, he expressly links the Church's zeal for souls with its devotion to St Joseph, whom he recognises as a leading source of its missionary impulse. The text in question reads: [5]

**"St Joseph's patronage must be invoked as ever necessary for the Church, not only as a defence against all dangers but also, and indeed primarily, as an impetus for her renewed commitment to evangelization in the world, as well as to re-evangelization in those lands and nations where religion and the Christian life were formerly flourishing but are now being put to a hard test."**

No one realises more keenly than the Redeemer's father and guardian what a price was paid for the salvation of souls. Etched indelibly in Joseph's memory were the angel's words: "You shall call him Jesus, for he will save his people from their sins" (Mt 1: 21). The sacred name officially imposed by Joseph on his legal Son says it all. Jesus is the Saviour of the world and died for each and every single person. Let us repeat this all-important truth: each and every single human being is precious beyond all earthly evaluations. Accordingly St Joseph is totally supportive of the Church's apostolic work—the work that brings into human destinies the Saviour's gospel of love and everlasting life.

**Nazareth in Space and Time**

It has been said that every branch of theology finds an echo in the mystery of Nazareth—the mystery of that holy house hold over which Joseph ruled with a father's love and care. Certainly the saying is richly verified when we theologise about the Church. For the Holy Family was its nucleus, its "first beginning." Hence, as we have seen, there was nothing arbitrary in the fact that St Joseph is venerated as the Church's univeral protector. Cardinal Suenens says in this connection: [6]

> **"Joseph's task remains identical through all the changes and chances of this life, and his patronage of the Church is but the prolongation of his historical mission. Since the days of Nazareth the family of God has been enlarged to the dimensions of the world, and St Joseph's heart has been enlarged to the measure of that new fatherhood which prolongs and surpasses that promised by God to Abraham, the father of many nations ... Joseph, the foster-father of Jesus, is such also of the brethren of Jesus—Christians down the ages. Husband of Mary, the mother of Jesus, he remains mysteriously united to her while the mystical birth of the Church pursues its course."**

### The Church in the Home

Because the family is the Church's basic unit, the very building block out of which it is composed, the Christian home has from earliest times been designated the domestic Church, the Church in miniature, the microcosm of the world-wide reality. And Joseph's Nazareth home is correspondingly seen as its prototype, model and inspiration. For a Christian home's whole vocation and goal is to mirror the exemplary faith and charity that prevailed in Joseph's household and to emulate it in every possible way.

Adrienne von Speyer saw very deeply into the connection and continuity between Nazareth and Christian families: [7]

> **"The Holy Family lived in Nazareth for us—the Christians of the future. Their Nazareth home is no**

**closed house, nor a closed paradise; it has doors and windows that open up into the Church."**

In his inspiring apostolic exhortation on the subject, John Paul II urges today's hard-pressed families to seek in[8] Joseph's family the help they need to be faithful to their duties, to bears life's trials and tribulations, to be open and generous towards others, and to fulfil joyfully God's will in all things. The pontiff identified the present-day "unchaste environment" as the chief source of danger for family life. The resultant evils include sexual licence, abortion, infidelity, divorce, the break-up of marriages and homes, and the damaging effects all this inevitably has on children.

The God-given lifeline for every Church in the home lies in prayer, especially prayer made jointly by family members. The celebrated slogan holds true for all times: "The family that prays together stays together." Devotion to St Joseph is particularly effective in solving domestic problems; not for nothing does the Church hail him in her litany as "the mainstay of families."

A form of family prayer particularly recommended is the rosary. By thus jointly honouring Joseph and Mary, the Christian family brings their beloved Son's abundant blessings into their home, making of it, in Paul VI's words, "a sanctuary of love and cradle of life." John Paul II recalled this golden expression when he wrote:[9]

**"Joseph and Mary are the summit from which holiness spreads all over the earth. The Saviour began the work of salvation by this virginal and holy union, wherein is manifested his all-powerful will to purify and sanctify the family—that sanctuary of love and cradle of life."**

### Joseph our Father

"To be a true son or daughter of St Joseph—the saint of our hearts, the glorious father of our life and our love." This was the ideal set by St Francis of Sales[10] for his spiritual children to emulate. It brings home to us two consoling truths: first, Joseph's love focuses upon every single person; and, secondly, his love is fatherly in mode.

In short, Joseph father-loves us, thus paralleling Mary's mother-love in our regard. Moreover, many mystics, including Teresa of Avila, Venerable Mother St Joseph (the first French Carmelite of the Reform), and Blessed Charles de Foucauld, testify that God has filled Joseph's heart with a father-love for us so immense and tender that it far exceeds anything we are familiar with on earth.

Among those who discovered St Joseph's father-love and treasured it thereafter as a pearl of great price was St Bernadette. Besides being homesick in her Nevers convent for her beloved Lourdes, she sorely missed her father, to whom she was affectionately attached. And when he was called from this world she was desolate with grief. It was at this point that she received through Our Lady the grace to see, ever so vividly, that from his place in heaven St Joseph would thenceforward fill the role in her life of an all-loving father. This new relationship become the light of Bernadette's spiritual life, inspiring her to live, to pray and to suffer as became a daughter of the saint who had transformed her Nevers convent into the holy house of Nazareth.

"St Joseph is my father and the patron saint of a holy death." This saying was frequently on St Bernadette's lips. How warmly she would have endorsed the exhortation addressed by Pope John XXIII to workers in Rome:[11]

> **"All the saints assuredly merit honour and particular respect. But it is evident that St Joseph possesses a just title to a more sweet, more intimate, more penetrating place in our hearts—a place that belongs to him alone."**

### Joseph Linked with Mary

Another feature of St Bernadette's spirituality is that she habitually linked Joseph and Mary in her devotions. There is a sound theological reason for this, as Bernardine of Siena[12] pointed out long before: the hearts of Joseph and Mary are so united that there exists between them an identity of love and interests. Furthermore, their lives are now even more closely bonded and interlocked in heaven than they were during the years when the redemptive drama was being played out on earth. Yet another factor accounting for their closeness is that every grace we receive through St Joseph's prayers comes to us, like all others, through his holy spouse, the Mediatrix of all Graces.

"We are quite confident," says Leo XIII[13] of the Mary-Joseph linking practice, "that this is what the Blessed Virgin herself would like." He particularly recommends that we add a prayer to St Joseph when we recite the rosary. In fact, he calls these "the inseparable prayers," their common purpose being that "God might be more willing to grant our petitions and aid his Church more promptly and generously."

Mention of rosary recalls the amazing sixth apparition at Fatima (October 13, 1917). In the first vision representing the rosary's joyful mysteries, the visionaries saw a red-cloaked St Joseph holding the Child; both were jointly blessing the world. What we are to read into this episode is Our Lady of the Rosary's wish that in these troubled times we pay a greater devotion than ever to her spouse, as well as combining and bonding it with devotion to herself.

The medieval theologian, John Gerson,[14] encourages us to adopt two practices which, he confidently asserts, will bring us untold blessings:

> **"Take St Joseph for your first patron, for your most intimate friend . . . Also, go to Mary through Joseph; assisted by so devoted a patron, so tender a mother, you will obtain from the heart of Jesus all your desires, for time and for eternity."**

As we would expect, a good many mystics have testified to the value and efficacy of conjoining our prayers to the Redeemer's earthly parents; indeed, it was in almost every instance the mother of God herself who recommended the practice. Both to Saint Gertrude and St Bridget she first proudly revealed her spouse's exceptional degree of glory before expressing her deep admiration and affection for him. And she confided to St John Eudes that Joseph was the first object of her love next to God, indicating that they were united in their intercession on our behalf. St Claude de la Colombiere, too, received a similar message from Our Lady. And of St Theresa of Lisieux it was said that her devotion to Mary and Joseph habitually went "in tandem."

As for her great Spanish namesake,[15] she related that once during an ecstasy the Blessed Virgin took her by the hand and thanked her for her great zeal in spreading devotion to St Joseph, whose loving intercession is so united with her own. St Francis of Sales was likewise convinced of Joseph's intercessory power, his reason being that "Our Blessed Lady and her glorious Son will refuse him nothing."[16]

## Spiritual Progress

Similarly a host of authorities testify to the power of St Joseph's intercession in promoting our spiritual lives, that is, our prayer-life and our practice of Christian virtues. This power arises in the first place from his privileged position as spouse of Mary and guardian of her Divine Son. Secondly, it is due to his own dazzling holiness as the "just man" whose all-round Christlikeness was surpassed only by that of Mary.

St Bernadette and Blessed Charles de Foucauld are among those devotees of Joseph who liken his fatherly authority and guidance to a spiritual Nazareth; there, as adopted brothers and sisters of Jesus, we learn to submit as he did to Joseph's paternal authority and duly grow in spiritual stature. Bernadette was aware of the general law, indeed imperative, of spiritual growth: "he who is holy must become holier still" (Apoc. 22: 11). But she may not have been aware of the intriguing circumstance that, in the original Hebrew, the name Joseph means "God will give growth."

Anyhow she placed all her strivings after true Christlikeness entirely in the hands of the saint who was her beloved father and spiritual master in heaven. We find the following entry in her personal notebook: [17]

**"In order that Jesus may grow, I must diminish. He will grow as much as I diminish. So grow in me, Jesus; grow as you did at Nazareth."**

Likewise with prayer—that indispensable nourisher of holiness. Herein the "just man" of Nazareth is the ideal instructor and guide, as Bernadette knew from personal experience. "When we do not know how to pray," she added to the above entry, "we must turn to Joseph."

Blessed Charles de Foucauld felt so strongly drawn to what he called the "spiritual Nazareth," that is, Joseph's supernatural world of humble obedience and prayer, that he went to live in the town itself, working as a floor-sweeper in the Poor Clare convent. "My vocation," he wrote, "is life in Nazareth." And there he came to appreciate the wise and helpful words of a priest-friend:[18]

**"Nazareth is where one works, where one obeys . . . It is a house one builds in one's heart; or rather, a house that one allows to be built in oneself by the hands of Jesus."**

### More Spiritual Progress

Not to be omitted in this context is Teresa of Avila's[19] warm endorsement of St Joseph's zeal and wonderful skill in promoting the spiritual life. "If anyone cannot find someone to teach him how to pray," she wrote, "let him take this glorious saint as his master and he will not go astray . . . I have never known anyone be truly devoted to him who did not notably advance in virtue."

Not to be omitted either is that other outstanding disciple of St Joseph—Francis of Sales.[20] He repeatedly assures us that the saint will reward our devotion by helping us grow to a marked degree in all the virtues. Now which virtue, we may ask, does our spiritual life stand most in need of at a practical level? St Francis has no hesitation in identifying it as peace of mind and heart—a quality so closely associated with St Joseph that it is virtually his trademark.

Finally, Joseph helps us to live habitually and closely in the presence of God. For he was one of that blessed trio who formed a "shadow of the Trinity" in their Nazareth home. There, in Newman's phrase,[21] "they opened up a communion of heavenly things" in which we the faithful are now privileged to participate.

That communion, which is in reality the Communion of Saints, will find its glorious consummation in the next world, our true homeland. Meanwhile St Joseph, the man of prayer and action, who embodies such qualities as security, faithfulness, stability, steadiness, perseverance, patience, confidence and trust, assists and guides us, day after day, on our pilgrimage of faith to the Holy Family's paradisal home, which will also be ours forever. To quote Newman once again:[22]

**"There is but one saint who typifies for us the next world, and that is St Joseph. He is the type of rest, repose, peace. He is the saint and patron of home, in death as well as in life."**

## REFERENCES FOR CHAPTER NINE
## DEVOTION TO ST JOSEPH

1...St Francis of Sales: Oeuvres Completes, VI, 369-370
2...Leo XIII: Quamquam Pluries
3...St Ambrose: In Lucam, 2, 1
4...Paul VI: Evangelii Nuntiandi
5...John Paul II: Redemptoris Custos, 29
6...Cardinal Leo J. Suenens: Mary, the Mother of God, pp 137-138
7...Adrienne von Speyer: Handmaid of the Lord, p. 92
8...John Paul II: Familiaris Consortio
9...John Paul II: Redemptoris Custos, 7 (Paul VI's expression here
      quoted is from his Discourse to the Equipes Notre-Dame
      Movement, May 4, 1970)
10..St Francis of Sales: Letter to St Jane de Chantal,
      March 19, 1614
11..John XXIII: Allocution on March 19, 1959
12..St Bernardine of Siena: Sermo de S.Josepho, 2, 1

13..Leo XIII: op. cit.

14..John Gerson: In Oratione Josephi

15..St Teresa of Avila: Autobiography, ch 33

16..St Francis of Sales: Discourse 19 in Oeuvres Completes, 19

17..St Bernadette: quoted by  A. Ravier in Les Ecrits de
     S. Bernadette, p 366

18..Father Huvelin: Letter to Bl. Charles de Foucauld, April 4, 1905

19..St Teresa of Avila: op. cit. ch 6

20..St Francis of Sales: op. cit. 6, pp 369-370

21..Cardinal John Henry Newman: Meditations and
     Devotions, p 14

22..Cardinal John Henry Newman: Sermon Notes, pp 203-204